The 3 Ms of
FEARLESS
DIGITAL
PARENTING

Proven Tools to Help You Raise Smart and Savvy Online Kids

CARRIE ROGERS-WHITEHEAD
founder of Digital Respons-Ability

Skyhorse Publishing

Skyhorse Publishing books may be purchased in bulk at special discounts for sales promotion, corporate gifts, fund-raising, or educational purposes. Special editions can also be created to specifications. For details, contact the Special Sales Department, Skyhorse Publishing, 307 West 36th Street, 11th Floor, New York, NY 10018 or info@skyhorsepublishing.com.

Skyhorse® and Skyhorse Publishing® are registered trademarks of Skyhorse Publishing, Inc.®, a Delaware corporation.

Visit our website at www.skyhorsepublishing.com.

10 9 8 7 6 5 4 3 2 1

Library of Congress Cataloging-in-Publication Data is available on file.

Cover design by Daniel Brount
Cover illustration by Shutterstock

Print ISBN: 978-1-5107-6372-2
Ebook ISBN: 978-1-5107-6373-9

Printed in the United States of America

For my parents, who supported my dreams and, through their example, helped make me a better digital parent.

Table of Contents

Chapter 1
Parenting without Fear

CARLY is afraid. She has two teenagers at home, each with their own phone. She has persistent, recurring thoughts about tech use in the home. She thinks that she made a mistake giving each of them a phone. (Are they too young for their own phones? Did they really need them?) She wonders what they are doing online. (Who are they talking to? Are they being bullied?) She worries that they aren't getting enough sleep or exercise. (When did they get to bed last night? Shouldn't they be outside more?) She frets about their grades this semester—and college admissions. She stresses about their social lives—and if she will ever be a grandma. Her thoughts consume the in-between spaces of the day. Sometimes she can't fall asleep. Sometimes she snaps at her teens. Sometimes she neglects her husband and friends.

I have seen other parents like Carly in my consulting work with parents. When I ask them about their concerns on the topic of digital parenting, their words spill out, barely contained. They worry about the past, present and future; they worry about their worries.

I get those worries too as a parent. Those little slithering thoughts that slide into my brain randomly through the day, but mostly at night when all is still. *Should I sign my kid up for a music class? I should be buying more vegetables. He was coughing last night, is he getting sick? I think he's growing out of his shoes.*

Parenting can be an ongoing monologue of things to do and think. The *shoulds* fill our brain and are difficult to shut off. It takes intense concentration and focus to reframe and mitigate those thoughts. Sometimes we're too tired to have a particular battle that day.

Why Are We Afraid?

Media Hyperbole

Here is a sampling of media headlines about technology in early 2020:

**"Local expert warns about dangers
of popular social media apps"**
—KSNT News

**"New online trend 'Outlet Challenge'
poses dangers and threat"**
—WITN News

**"Protecting your kids from child predators: how police
investigate and what parents can do"**
—KOKH FOX 25 News

**"Parents warned of dangers as TikTok skull
breaker challenge goes viral"**
—Independent Online

**"They coerced girls on Instagram, Snapchat to send
sexually explicit images, police say"**
—The Modesto Bee

"4 social media scams that could cost you"
—KSL News

That last headline was mine, but I didn't choose it, my editor did. Headlines are very specifically written to get attention. I can suggest headlines as the author—but my suggestions are not as popular. It would more accurately be titled "Strategies to keep your money safe." But you wouldn't know that from the headline.

Here's another article headline: "If your kids are using anonymous messaging app Lipsi, they probably shouldn't." This is from a piece I wrote in late 2018 that I originally titled the very straightforward "Lipsi App review." But that wouldn't get hits.

Headlines are misleading, but we can't just blame the media for this, we have to point the finger at ourselves. People want their news fast and free. People are also inundated with news. There is increasing competition for eyes and clicks. And there is an increased workload for editors and journalists.

Take my editor on KSL, for example. She has to oversee not only the tech section, but also family and religion. Her duties also include responding to breaking events, helping out other news departments, editing contributors' articles, researching her own pieces, and posting multiple times a day on social media. It's a huge workload. If you're already overworked, you're going to spend the most time on the stories that get the most views.

If I can get double the hits on a piece for something scary and titillating, I'm going to do that. But because I'm not a full-time journalist, I can afford to write on more esoteric topics like digital inclusion. I remember a few years ago I spent many hours interviewing and writing up a well-researched article on what my city is doing to aid in digital inclusion. I was very proud, but the article did not get very many views.

The most popular article I've written for KSL as of now was one about the dark web. My other most popular stories are app reviews or stories of tech trends typically with a oh-no-what-is-this-new-thing slant. Scary and sensational sells, so we write more scary or sensational headlines. It's basic supply and demand—people demand more fear-based articles, so journalists deliver. If my well-researched and tech-positive digital inclusion story got more views, there would be more requests for me to write that type of piece.

Just because there are *more* scary headlines doesn't mean that there are *more* scary apps or tech out there. We're only seeing one side of the story. And we're not always reading the whole story. If you read deeply into my Lipsi article, near the end I write about some pros of the app. But you would never know that if you just read the headline.

Modern-Life Anxieties

Work stress and lack of leisure time can affect our physical and mental health. In the United States alone, there are no federal laws that limit the maximum length of the workweek. There are also no laws requiring paid sick days or maternity leave. (The US is the only industrialized country in the entire world that has no legally mandated leave.) In the United States, 85.8 percent of men and 66.5 percent of women work more than 40 hours a week. We are overworked. We are tired. It's harder to calm our brains and fears when we are running from one thing to another.

When you go to work, you're told what time to get there, what tasks to perform, when you can leave, what you can and can't wear, and much more. We do not have much control over our work life. We have bosses and responsibilities and bills. When we feel out of control in the workplace, we may try even harder to control what we can in our home life, such as making sure dinner is perfect, or the house looks "just so." Maybe we become more vigilant about our own calorie counts or spending. Perhaps it comes out in our parenting.

This book will ask a lot of self-reflective questions to help you think about your parenting. Not only to answer the question: "How can I get my child to comply?" but also "Why is this important to me?" Are you creating rules and boundaries about technology because it's important for you to be in control, because you feel uncomfortable around your own tech use, or because technology truly is impacting your family life?

In a 2019 longitudinal study of adolescents in South Korea, Christopher Ferguson, a professor of psychology at Stetson University, spoke bluntly about the results. "It was the parents' fault," he said in our interview. "Parents were pushing kids to be academically successful so hard and they broke their kids." In South Korea, testing is huge, and there is an enormous emphasis on educational attainment. A former history teacher in Seoul describes the culture:

> South Korea is a Confucian-inspired society that places an immense value on education, which is both admirable and exemplary. From kindergarten onward, Korean students are shuttled off to private academies for additional instruction and studies. This continues even after the end of each school day and frequently extends to weekends and holidays as well.

This pressure, while well-meaning, has had unfortunate side effects. South Korea has a high suicide rate for secondary students. South Korea is also home to an increasing number of young people described as "gaming addicts."

That's what the parents in the research study said—their kids were gaming addicts. "Those parents wanted to say that this was a disease in their kids, but the data showed that it was the parents' fault," said Ferguson.

The parents' anxieties and fears about college, career, and success were transferred to those students. The stressed-out teens were using gaming to cope with their parents' anxieties and fears—and then being labeled "addicts."

Modern life is stressful enough. We don't need to pass its stresses on to our children.

Generational Fears

Another question to ask along with "Why is this important to me?" is "Remember when you were a teenager?" It's easy to forget that we were all teenagers. We may have even blocked out parts of it. My own adolescence was a time of extreme ups and downs, tears and triumphs. I can look back at it now through a nostalgic haze which blurs the details. I suspect many of you look back at your younger years through that same haze. We forget how things were, how *we* were. New things are unfamiliar, not glossed over with that shiny haze of memory. It's this haze that colors our perceptions of the current generation.

There are generational anxieties even between parents. Gen Xers, millennials, and older Gen Zers are all parenting children now. Each of those three generations grew up differently. Anna Dees, a self-described "cusper" born in 1978 said that she feels a disconnect with other parents. She noted, "It's really interesting to see the ones who have grown up with video games and Internet and Myspace and they're putting their kids on Snapchat." Anna feels like the mean mom with rules for technology that are stricter than those of her younger neighbors. "There's a different result in my parenting perspective and how I'm parenting versus some of the younger moms. I think some of the Gen Xers and Gen Zers have different perspectives. There are some things that are normalized in their culture that have become jarring to me."

Our generational anxieties are nothing new. A famous quote attributed to the Greek philosopher Socrates in about 400 BC reads: "The children now love luxury; they have bad manners, contempt for authority; they show disrespect for elders and love chatter in place of exercise. Children are now tyrants, not the servants of their households."

That quote could have come straight out of the 2020s.

There have always been fears of new things and younger generations. One example is the 1993 video game Doom that features a first-person shooter. (Today, you have better graphics on your phone than that original Doom, but in 1993 it was extremely advanced tech.) The popularity of this game compelled experts and educators to go on the news spreading their fears. Reed Irvine and Cliff Kincaid commented on this phenomenon in their 1999 think piece "Video Games Can Kill":

By now, you may be aware of this video game, whose effects have been highlighted on the CBS *60 Minutes* program and the NBC *Today Show*. On both shows, a former army colonel described the game as a "mass murder simulator" that provides military-type training. He said it is like the flight simulators that teach military personnel how to fly aircrafts. In fact, *60 Minutes* showed how the video game Doom is used in the military itself to teach soldiers how to kill. In the game, the gunman moves slowly through a building, in the same way that a special forces soldier might enter hostile territory. Enemies are shot and killed, as simulated blood spatters out of their wounds and they fall to the ground in pools of blood. In the Kentucky case, the young killer, fourteen-year-old Michael Carneal, had never undergone any firearms training. He learned how to shoot and kill from the video game. When he walked into the bible study meeting at his high school with a gun, he proceeded to shoot his victims with deadly accuracy.

You may think, "but compared to back then, technology is different," and you'd be both right and wrong. Technology is different, but the human behind the screen is pretty similar. We are a bundle of fears, motivations, hormones, and experiences. While the technology may change from a commodore to a supercomputer, or a bronze sword to a video game, the human behind it is the same.

Every generation has fears. One generation is afraid of the radio, the other the horse-drawn carriage. It's important to keep in mind that your parents were afraid of what you were doing. And their parents were afraid for your parents. It's normal to have these generational gaps. But if you operate only with fears, you will not only risk having a quote posted on a web archive somewhere embarrassing you, but you can also cause unintentional harm.

Awareness versus Understanding

One thing that is different about our current generation is our awareness of what's happening all the time. News reports, social media, and our interconnected 24-7 society allows us to be hyperaware of the world around us. This awareness does not alleviate our fears. Fear does not come from lack of awareness but from lack of understanding.

The unfamiliar and new are hard to understand. Being shut out of young people's online spaces and their conversations guarded by passwords makes us nervous. If you're reading this book, you're probably aware of the issues; you just don't understand them. If you don't understand the new rules of communication and etiquette, what it's like to be a kid today, or the algorithms in your apps, this book will attempt to build a bridge of understanding.

Technology is new and different, and we don't see clearly through the fog of time. The media exacerbates this. And the day-to-day stresses only add to our growing pile of worries. All of this creates a culture of panic, worry, anxiety, depression, and fear around digital parenting. This book includes many questions and *shoulds* and *woulds*, but I hope to narrow down and dismiss some of those fears—to look past the headlines into the data.

Being a parent means having a monologue in your head. Carly has that repetitive script and so do I. We're attuned to our kids. We care. But that well-meaning caring can hurt us both and our children if we're not careful. We'll discuss some of those harms later in this book. For now, let's cross off some tech fears on our to-do list and put our energy where it really counts.

Chapter 2
The 3 Ms of Digital Parenting

IN 2017 I had just started talking to parents about technology. My company, Digital Respons-Ability, first started teaching students digital citizenship until I realized we needed to teach parents too. It started small, in conversations and conferences, and I observed quickly that parents seemed to be operating with different expectations and feelings about technology. It was okay for a child to be in their room alone and read, but not text. Board games were great, but video games were looked down upon.

Another disconnect was understanding where children were developmentally. A parent wouldn't expect their preschooler to be the best dinner companion, but they did chide them for watching too much TV. A mother would be fine with their teen hanging out at a park with their friends but would remark that they texted their friends excessively. Technology seemed to be treated as this separate part of parenting with its own set of rules.

From these observations and conversations, one of my company's trainers and I developed "The 3 Ms of Digital Parenting" because we realized that discussions about technology need to have a science-based framework. Parents were making decisions about technology in the home by treating it as a separate entity that was independent from where that child was socially, emotionally, and biologically. But all parenting, including digital parenting, needs to take into account the age and understanding of the child.

The 3 M's of
DIGITAL PARENTING

Developmental stages are times in a child's development when certain abilities appear and include domains such as physical, cognitive, language, and social-emotional development. Adults go through these developmental stages as well, but children's are shorter and much more pronounced. Understanding your child's developmental stages not only helps you parent more effectively but can also help you screen for developmental delays that call for interventions.

One well-known developmental screening tool is the Ages & Stages Questionnaires® (ASQ®). Developed over forty years ago by experts and recommended by the American Academy of Pediatrics and the Center for Disease Control, ASQ® can help parents "celebrate their child's milestones and know what to look for next." I used this tool with my own child from birth to age five. As someone who thought herself very familiar with early childhood stages through reading books and from personal experiences, I discovered that I had more to learn. For example, how a child throws a ball, gestures to objects, and picks up toys can reveal more about where they are developmentally.

The 3 Ms of Digital Parenting framework is not intended to be a screening tool, but rather a framework to create healthy norms of behavior in the home—to understand what to pay more attention to, and what to let go of. Understanding what not to worry about is an important part of parenting. It's something I've had to work on with my son. I loved reading at a young age so I was fretting that my son wasn't reading enough and that he was falling behind. But after talking to his teacher and reading more on the subject, I realized that he was just fine. I was projecting my own experiences and unrealistic expectations onto him. He's his own person with his own interests and strengths.

As parents, we often project our own pasts and experiences onto our children because it's our framework for viewing the world. We are excited when they love the same books or movies as we did as kids. If we did sports, we want them play. If we were musical, we encourage them to pick up an instrument.

Technology, however, was not the same experience when we were children. We cannot project our analog past on their digital present. We need to understand where children *are*, not where we want them to be. This means looking at their technology use through a different lens, not through our past, but through evidence-based research.

The 3 Ms of Digital Parenting framework shares research, advice, and strategies into different developmental stages: Model, ages 0–8; Manage, ages 8–13; and Monitor, ages 13–18. This book uses both this framework and one of prevention science to truly see our children as they are. Frameworks are deliberately fuzzy as a way to guide your thinking, but not tell you what to think. Parenting involves operating in that fuzzy and grey area.

Dr. Sarah Coyne is a professor of human development who researches the effects of technology on young people. Some of her insights and research will be shared in this book. When talking to her, both of us acknowledged that grey area and the challenges. "I think our job is to help kids become healthy users of media," Dr. Coyne said. "It doesn't mean we completely limit it or give them free rein. It's a challenge and something we're constantly working at." Even experts acknowledge the challenges. It's not easy but if we can shift our way of looking at the problems, we can more easily find the best solutions.

Model (Ages 0–8)

We change more biologically in our early years than any other time in life. It's estimated by Harvard's Center on the Developing Child that more than one million new neural connections form every second in our first few years of life. After that rapid growth of connections, our brain focuses on efficiency and prunes them. We continue learning, but those early years provide a foundation. Parents can add to that foundation by providing "responsive caregiving" and attention to their children and modeling positive behaviors. More details about this dynamic time of growth will be explored in Chapter 3 on page 25.

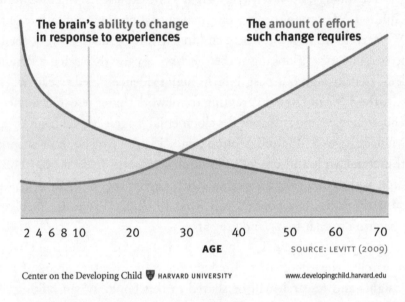

The brain's ability to change in response to experiences

The amount of effort such change requires

2 4 6 8 10   20   30   40   50   60   70

AGE   SOURCE: LEVITT (2009)

Center on the Developing Child 🛡 HARVARD UNIVERSITY   www.developingchild.harvard.edu

In my digital parenting classes, I focus on several concepts during this stage: vocabulary, creating norms and habits, self-regulation, and screen time. While these concepts are important at other developmental stages, they're critical in these years.

Vocabulary

Laurieann Thorpe is the executive director of Prevent Child Abuse Utah (PCAU) and a mother of three. She explains why teaching vocabulary to children is so important:

> When a child has been sexually abused, they do not have the tools they need to disclose the abuse when they don't know the correct names for their body parts. Teaching children the anatomically correct names of their body parts empowers

them to talk about what is happening to them and research shows that it also empowers them against abuse.

To keep children safe online, children should not only know the names of their body parts, but also have a vocabulary for technology. If a child saw something online that made them uncomfortable, a parent should know how that happened. This means a child needs to communicate words like "website, click, download, app, pop-up," and the names of platforms like YouTube and other games that they're playing. If a parent knows how the inappropriate content came about, they can adjust settings and controls so that it doesn't happen again. Thorpe goes on to explain the importance of teaching children the tools needed to communicate. "Imagine if they went to the doctor after spraining an ankle and explained that they hurt their 'walkie?' You can see how that would be confusing."

Young children are typically not deliberately seeking inappropriate content. That comes later when puberty hits and they become more curious and interested in what their friends think. Preadolescents typically have the vocabulary to express and find content online, but young children do not, and may stumble upon things accidentally. They may not have the words to describe what they are seeing or how they found it, but parents can give them that voice.

Creating Norms and Habits

Norms, rituals, habits, routines—these are the concepts around which we scaffold our lives. Parents start routines early: feeding, sleeping, stories, play, etc. We develop these routines and norms both by necessity, and to pass along our values to our children. For example, a parent who is religious may say a prayer before dinner. The routine of praying is both routine and ritual and a way a parent transmits their beliefs to their child. An article in the *Infants & Young Children* journal writes:

> During the early childhood years, family routines afford
> the opportunity for engaging children in dyadic and group

activities that have been shown to contribute to vocabulary enrichment, social skill building, and later academic *achievement* . . . family routines under relatively normative conditions appear to be part of the organizational and predictable parts of family life that support child development.

While families are establishing routines around meals, recreation, and sleep, they're also creating their own technology norms. This may be watching TV after dinner, or Friday night movies, or tablets in the car. You probably had your own technology routines as a child. Maybe it was Saturday morning cartoons or playing video games after school. I remember one of mine was gathering together as a family on Sunday nights and watching the newest episode of *The X-Files*.

We don't always consciously establish routines, but if we do, we can make sure our habits align with our values. We should question our routines and adjust them as circumstances change. Ask yourself: Is this habit the best use of my family's time? Do my children still enjoy doing this? If I care about _____ does this routine address that?

Self-Regulation

I remember hearing a comment from a parent, "My six-year-old never wants to get off YouTube!" To which I think, *Why* would *you think your six-year-old could get off YouTube themselves?* Children are doing the hard work of learning self-regulation at this age. The bright shiny noises and objects on YouTube are very hard for a young child to ignore.

Self-regulation continues our whole lives but is particularly important in young children. The foundational skills for self-regulation are developed in the first five years of life. This starts in infancy when an infant may suck a binky if they are scared. A preschooler may reach out to a soft toy to soothe themselves in a new situation. And we see adults self-regulating by scrolling Instagram.

Technology can be a tool to help children soothe themselves, but it can also be a substitute for their own internal work of self-regulation.

Tech can help us tune out when we don't want to tune into our own internal worlds. A device can be a distraction from emotions that need to be experienced or can increase arousal instead of calm. Parents can model self-regulation by such actions as:

- Asking questions of their child and awaiting a response.
    "What do you think of the book?"
- Calling attention to things.
    "Do you see that kid over there? Do you want to invite them to play with you?"
- Helping them recognize emotions.
    "I wonder if you're upset." "I'm here for you if you need help."

Screen Time

Screen time is a hot topic with parents that will be explored in several chapters of this book. The evidence behind screen time surveys is flawed and we lack longitudinal research. The *Journal of Child Psychology and Psychiatry* published a metanalysis of these screen time surveys in 2020 and found that "most research to date has been correlational, focused on adults versus adolescents, and has generated a mix of often conflicting small, positive, negative, and null associations."

While studies around older children and adolescents are murkier, it's clearer with infants. One 2019 longitudinal study published in the *Journal of the American Medical Association* found that more time per week spent on screens by two-year-olds resulted in worse performance on screening tests that looked at behavioral, cognitive, and social development by age three. In fact, dozens of studies have found that infants and toddlers consistently learn better from face-to-face learning than from someone on the screen. The person on the screen can be doing the exact same thing but very young children don't translate that learning into real life. This is called the "transfer deficit" and research published in the *Journal of Experimental Psychology* also sees this deficit in interactive apps.

Parents should severely limit screen time under age three. This, of course, is difficult. I've broken this rule. When my child was a toddler the YouTube Kids app allowed me to have enough alone time to get a shower in the morning. I also relied on a combination of blocks and Baby TV to do those tasks necessary for life: cleaning, cooking, taking a minute to myself, etc. But parents should understand and enforce limits on screen time at early ages.

Manage (Ages 8–13)

The preadolescent or "tween" years are a critical time of change. Like young children, tweens' bodies are rapidly evolving, but unlike young children, they care more about peers than parents. The biological and social changes of these ages will be explored more in Chapter 4 on page 49. When talking to parents of tweens, I address the concepts of public information, personal boundaries and privacy, digital etiquette, and creating an environment of trust.

Public Information

Older children are beginning to create their own online presence or digital footprint. As parents, we should guide them on what information is appropriate to share. Each platform has different requirements for what is needed to create an account. If possible, use your own contact information when signing up your children for sites. You can also consider creating a generic email address for your child that is attached to your own.

Table 2.1 Public versus Private Information Online

Public Information	Private Information
Name (Some sites require this; others just want a username.)	Location
Public profile picture	Other pictures of yourself
Username	Your contacts
Bio (Some sites require this, others do not. If it is required, keep it short and vague.)	Interests, hobbies, saved links, and videos
Public IP address (a.k.a Internet IP)	Financial information

Personal Boundaries and Privacy

Along with protecting privacy through what is shared online, children need to create their own boundaries at this age. Unlike in early childhood, children at these ages are, and should be, interacting independently from their parents. They will not necessarily have a parent to step in and protect them; they are the ones that must step up. When children are online, they need to understand that they can, and should, say no, delete accounts, report incidents, and take a break when interactions happen online that make them feel uncomfortable.

Laurieann Thorpe describes this boundary-setting process in her work with Prevent Child Abuse Utah:

> One of the first things we teach children is that their bodies belong to them. We teach the youngest of children to listen to their feelings, say "no," and go tell. They need the same permission to protect their privacy. They do not necessarily have a right to privacy from their parents, especially when it comes to what they are doing online. In fact, a parent needs to understand and guide a child as they navigate social media, online gaming, smart phones, etc. As children grow, they need continued support as their online footprints grow with them.

The term "manage" at these ages means that parents must be more involved in their child's online lives, and that their child will have less online privacy. Part of that management process means teaching them about boundaries and giving them the tools, whether through role play, showing online moderation tools, or sharing scripts to help their child protect themselves.

When I taught my young son about his body, I would reiterate, "No one can touch you without your permission, and you need to ask permission to touch others." I would not just say this, however. I would demonstrate it. I would, and still do, ask, "Can I give you a hug?" or "Are you okay if I cuddle you?" I remember seeing my efforts pay off when he was four. We had walked to the door of his preschool class one morning. Our ritual was that I would ask him for a hug, and he would hug me at the door. For the first time, he turned me down; no hug. At first, I was a little shocked, and a bit sad, but then I smiled. The lessons had sunk in and now he was practicing them himself.

Just like with bodily autonomy, parents and caregivers should encourage online autonomy. I know my efforts in teaching online privacy will pay off when one day he will say, "No, Mom, I won't share that with you."

Digital Etiquette

My parents like to jokingly tell me the story of when I was a toddler, and they took me out to eat at a fancy restaurant. The restaurant had rich food, white tablecloths, and gleaming silverware—and I was having none of it. Apparently, I leapt onto the top of that gleaming white tablecloth and started throwing things. My parents left red-faced then but have laughed red-faced now about the hilarity of the situation.

A toddler has no etiquette. They will burp, scream, get messy, and sometimes throw food at fancy restaurants. A toddler has no etiquette in part because of where they are developmentally, but also because they have not been taught. The norms of eating out are foreign to them.

My parents have remarked that, in hindsight, taking a toddler to a fancy restaurant was a dumb idea. But many parents would not question taking a child to a digital location. While there is no risk of soiled linens online, digital spaces have their own etiquette and rules. Just like the unrealistic expectation that a toddler can identify a salad fork, we shouldn't have the same expectation that children know how to interact properly, politely, and safely in an online space. We must teach them digital etiquette. As with teaching food etiquette, parents must patiently explain why we do some things and not others, what online platforms (like forks) are used for certain tasks, and how we can communicate our needs to others online (like servers).

Creating an Environment of Trust

Tweens are rapidly turning the corner to teenagerhood, then adulthood. There are lots of road hazards on the way to adulthood, which means that parents must create an environment of trust. Tweens should know that they can always talk to their parents about their online lives. They should understand that their parents will keep their confidences, and trust that their parents will advocate for and protect them.

Trust isn't built in a day. It takes conversations, experiences, and "trust falls" or mistakes. Children make mistakes online, but they should trust that their parents are there to catch them, not shame them. The trust built through these preadolescent years serves as the foundation for the sometimes-rocky road of adolescence.

Monitor (Ages 13–18)

When I teach digital parenting classes, I sometimes use the analogy of the 3 Ms as a leash. When children are young, they need a firmer hand, like a puppy does. A puppy, like an infant, may get themselves in danger unknowingly, or eat things that make them sick. But as children age, that leash needs to lengthen. They're growing and learning and becoming more independent. They need more room to explore. When children reach adolescence, they need even more slack and room. They are only a few years away from leaving the home. At this age, their activities should be monitored but intervention should be used sparingly and only in serious situations. In addition to monitoring, another "M" word for teenagers is "mentor." Parents shift their role from teacher to coach. While teens need instruction (although they may not say it), they especially need support, mentorship, and love.

More information about digital parenting for teens will be shared in Chapter 5 on page 65. This book will also discuss removing that leash for adolescents in Chapter 9 on page 197. When my staff and I teach digital parenting classes to parents of teens we focus on four concepts: digital commerce, digital footprint, self-efficacy, and online creation versus consumption.

Digital Commerce (eCommerce)

Digital commerce, also known as eCommerce, are "commercial transactions that take place electronically online." It's estimated that by 2021 they will generate more than $4.5 trillion in sales per year. This area only continues to grow, with Nasdaq estimating that 95 percent of purchases will be digital by 2040.

Youth are part of this huge market, selling, buying, trading, and more, but with little instruction or help. Reported by *The New York Times*, only twenty-one states currently require high school students to take financial literacy. While this number has grown in recent years, it still means that many teens reach adulthood with little to no education around finances. That lack of knowledge is reflected in a financial literacy study by the National Center for Education Statistics, which said that "roughly 1 in 5 US 15-year-olds don't understand basic financial concepts." This lack of financial literacy, in addition to having a teen brain and less life experience, can lead young people to fall for scams or overspend. Another big financial issue for teens is online gaming purchases, discussed more in Chapter 7 on page 133. Parents can provide instruction and advice on financial literacy, and our teens definitely need it.

Digital Footprint

Anyone online creates a digital footprint. This can range from comments, cookies, posts, saved links, messages, and much more. That digital footprint can follow a person years later, either positively or negatively. There are countless examples from the news of a tweet or a comment that can come back to effect someone's job or relationship years later. I've heard the term "digital footprint" called a "digital billboard" because in some situations inappropriate comments can be broadcast widely like a billboard.

During adolescence, teens are moving into an adult world, but with teen brains. They are being Googled and evaluated by admissions officers and potential employers. Their digital footprint can be a plus or a minus for their future. I've told teens that I wish this wasn't the case; I wish they could live their teen years without worrying that what they say or do online will haunt them later. I feel for them; long-term thinking and planning is biologically harder for teens because their prefrontal cortex isn't fully developed. An ephemeral thought becomes permanent online. I've talked to many adults who are grateful that there was no social media until later in their lives. It's not fair for teens, but it is the reality of the world we live in. Thus, parents must mentor their children to look ahead and put themselves in the shoes of their future interviewer.

Self-Efficacy

I was raised in the 1990s when self-esteem was something continually talked about in classrooms. I was taught that if I believed in myself, I could achieve anything. While this is a pleasant thought, it's a lie. You can't just believe in yourself; you have to believe that you have control over your actions and responsibility for your feelings. You have to focus and work to achieve new skills. Believing is just the first step to achieving; it won't get you there alone.

Albert Bandura, described as the "greatest living psychologist," created the theoretical construct of self-efficacy. It is the belief that one can achieve their goals. Bandura found that people with high self-efficacy are more likely to view hard tasks as something to be mastered, rather than avoided. They're also more motivated to complete tasks, and if they fail, they will not shame or blame themselves, but examine the external factors contributing to that failure. Individuals with high self-efficacy also have higher self-control, and the more they master, the more that self-efficacy grows.

This is a difficult concept to teach. It requires parents, teachers, and others to stand by and let the student try, and sometimes fail. You have to develop self-efficacy by experience, not slogans from the 1990s about "believing in yourself." Parents can encourage this development by giving their teen space to explore and by not blaming technology for any failures. A parent should not say, "If you'd get off the phone, you'd do better in class," but rather something like, "You told me you wanted a better grade, is playing on your phone helping you reach that goal?" Teens must understand that they are in control of their own Internet and device use. Understanding that they are in control helps guide them to better decision-making, and ultimately achieving their goals.

Creation, Not Consumption

Related to the concept of self-efficacy, parents should encourage their teens to create, make, explore, and do, not simply consume content. They must shift their mindset from looking at the Internet as a danger, to a tool. There are still dangers online, more of which will be explored in Chapter 6 on page 93. Still, those dangers should not hold teens back from using online tools in a proactive, positive, and constructive way.

The flip side of online dangers are opportunities in the digital economy. A 2020 report out of the Berkman Klein Center for Internet & Society at Harvard describes the relationships between youth and the Internet through "capital-enhancing activities" or CEAs such as friendship, reputation, money, followers, status, or cultural capital. These are different than "recreational activities" like scrolling feeds, playing a game by yourself, or passively reading. "CEAs are digital practices that have tangible outcomes," according to the report, and they "also allow youth to exercise their agency and express their individuality and independence." So, teens are establishing their identities through their digital footprints. Creating and making online is part of that process. Parents can monitor and mentor their child from the sidelines, and one day applaud their teen's accomplishments.

Using This Framework

The famous developmental psychologist Jean Piaget described "magical thinking" as the belief that your ideas and thoughts can influence the events in the outside world. I remember observing this in my own child, who believed that his "stufties" (stuffed animals) prevented any scary dreams. Research suggests that young children do engage in this thinking but have more understanding than Piaget thought.

It's also found that adults, like children, engage in magical thinking. Some of this magical thinking may be unrealistic expectations or behaviors of our children. We may think, *If I take my child's phone away, this behavior will stop!* But behavior is caused by many factors and is not simply a straight line.

Understanding developmental stages mitigates magical thinking by grounding our expectations in biological reality. Looking at our children where they are developmentally keeps us from getting disappointed or frustrated when they don't act the way we want and prevents us from imposing our own beliefs and assumptions about their behavior. Those frustrations and disappointments affect our children. Even infants can sense negative moods from their caregivers. Over time that negativity can become toxic and make your child's behavior worse, creating a self-defeating and toxic cycle. If you are in that cycle, taking a step back, putting slack on the leash, and spending more time listening to and observing your child can replace unhealthy digital parenting patterns with more realistic biological and social/emotional solutions.

Chapter 3
The First M: Model
(Ages 0–8)

I used to have a pair of glittery gold sunglasses. They were cheap but I loved them because they were so comfy. This pair lived a long life, avoiding the common deaths of sunglasses: sitting on them in the car, losing them, etc. I wore them frequently and my then-toddler son became fixated on them. Can you blame him for the fixation? Not only were they shiny, but they were also something that his mother touched, handled, and used. He would reach for them and put them on, although not always correctly.

You may have an object of fixation in your home. Maybe it's your car keys or a favorite pair of earrings that your infant reaches for. When we use, touch, manipulate, and hold something it's sending a message to our children that this thing is important. It's why you see car keys made into colorful plastic toys, or

phones made into toddler-friendly versions. Children, even when nonverbal, are watching and observing and modeling our behavior. They mimic us in our expressions, mannerisms, favorite activities, and technology use. When a child continually reaches for a phone or tablet, what is that saying about our own tech usage?

This chapter will cover the first M of the 3 Ms of Fearless Digital Parenting: Model. Parents are their children's first teachers. Later, their peers will be the ones watched, but from birth to around age eight, they are mostly being taught by us. This is an opportunity to educate on important values and skills and set them up for healthy technology use.

In this chapter, we will discuss four important concepts to teach children aged 0–8: vocabulary, creating norms/rituals, self-regulation, and screen time. In my digital parenting classes, I talk about modeling behaviors not as a one-sided activity, but a back-and-forth process. Parents and caregivers need to self-reflect on their own digital behaviors. What are your objects of fixation, your shiny sunglasses? What behaviors are you consciously and unconsciously modeling for your child? At the end of this chapter, we will consider the steps needed to evaluate apps and select media for young children.

Vocabulary

When young children find inappropriate content, they typically stumble upon it by accident. And when this happens, they need the vocabulary to express what happened. It's difficult to protect and prevent when you as a parent don't know what happened. By giving your child the words to describe what they're seeing and experiencing online, you give them tools to keep themselves safe.

In my previous background as a youth services librarian, I taught early literacy at schools and organizations. I would visit schools and nonprofits to demonstrate these concepts by singing songs, doing finger plays, and dancing in front of adults. My early literacy training encouraged parents to help their children prepare to read by following five practices from the research-based initiative Every Child

Ready to Read (http://everychildreadytoread.org) which teach children new words and sounds. I feel that these practices are ideal for teaching any vocabulary for young children, even the vocabulary of the online world.

The five practices include Read, Write, Talk, Sing, and Play. They can start at birth and prepare infants and young children to later learn phonics, letters, words, and sentences. Here are some ways you can use these early literacy principles to prepare young children not only for reading but talking to adults about what they see and do online.

Read: Read books and articles about technology. Ask open-ended questions while you read (such as "What do you think will happen next?"). Some picture books for preschoolers around the topic of technology to read include:

- *#Goldilocks: A Hashtag Cautionary Tale* by Jeanne Willis
- Girls Who Code series by Josh Funk
- *Dot.* by Randi Zuckerberg
- *hello! hello!* by Matthew Cordell

Write: Model writing and typing for your children. Show your child that words can appear on a screen by pressing a keyboard. Let them see how you can type words in a search bar or in a document. Show them that a computer is used to write and read.

Talk: Describe what you are doing on your phone, tablet, or computer. Talk out loud while you work or search for something online. Even if you're not at a computer, continually talk to your children, point out objects or activities around you both, and narrate your day-to-day life. For example, instead of just saying "Eat your dinner" to a toddler you can say, "Use your spoon to pick up your peas for dinner."

Sing: Because songs have a lot of rhyming or more complex words, singing can help children learn that there are different sounds or phonics to each word. Each note in a song connects to a syllable, so although it may feel silly, instead of talking when performing tasks, sing instead. Or simply talk in a singsong voice to young children.

Play: This may be one of the easier and more fun ways of teaching new words to children. Let them play games on your tablet or phone occasionally. However, supervise them when you do and use vocabulary words as you explain how to play the game (i.e., click on that icon to give a command to the computer). Suggestions for apps and games to play with young children will be shared at the end of this chapter.

Remote learning is both an opportunity and a challenge for parents in teaching children safe and responsible technology use. Since the COVID-19 pandemic, more schools have moved to remote and online learning. As a result, many young children are being introduced to the Internet and technology without the proper instruction, scaffolding, and vocabulary to use it properly. Online homework is a good opportunity for parents to teach these vocabulary words to their children and have discussions with them about what to do when they see something scary.

Vocabulary for Young Children (Toddlers to Grade 2)
Here are some suggestions of vocabulary words to teach to young children. When I've taught digital citizenship to elementary students, I focus on these words:

- **Click (verb)**: The act of pushing a button, key, or icon to give a computer a command.
- **Pop-up**: A website that appears on your screen without being requested.
- **Permission**: The act of asking for an adult to okay your online time.

- **Screen**: Any device that has an electronic display including computers, tablets, phones, smart TVs, and more.
- **Device**: Electronic equipment used to perform commands.
- **Bullying**: The act of repeatedly saying/doing hurtful things to another person.
- **Internet permanence/Digital footprint**: The notion that everything you put on the Internet can stay there forever. What you do online can be seen by others.
- **Post**: A digital communication usually publicly displayed on social media.
- **Reply**: A comment on someone's post.
- **React**: Using words or an emoji to express your feelings about another person's post.
- **Emoji**: A cartoon picture that might be used in place of words or gestures.
- **Meme**: A picture with words on it. Memes communicate in two ways since both the picture and the words have meaning. A meme can also be thought of as a visual way to express an idea or belief.
- **GIF**: A very short video clip shared online.
- **Feed**: A page on a social media account that shows what other people have been posting.

Vocabulary for Older Children (Grade 2 to Grade 5)

This is a list of vocabulary that I've used with older children. Most of these words relate to the process of computational thinking, a problem-solving skill that requires students to think abstractly. It takes a complicated problem and breaks it down into potential solutions that can be understood by computers. To be clear, computational thinking is not coding, but the first step to coding and programming. Younger children may have difficulty grasping these more advanced concepts, but older children and tweens can.

- **Program (verb)**: The act of writing code for a computer.

- **Coding**: The language computers use to communicate.
- **Command**: The individual instruction given to a computer.
- **Algorithm**: More than one command given to a computer to do a specific action.
- **Bug**: A digital mistake in the algorithm.
- **Conditional**: An "if, then" statement for a computer (i.e., if you hear start, start moving, and if you hear stop, stop moving).
- **Event**: The command or algorithm that triggers a conditional.
- **Digital ethics**: Doing the right thing online.
- **Copyright**: The rights that a creator has to the work they produce and publish.

Norms and Rituals

Author of the child development book, *The Gardener and the Carpenter: What the New Science of Child Development Tells Us About the Relationship Between Parents and Children*, Alison Gopnik writes about how modeling occurs:

> We take it for granted that children learn from their parents and other caregivers . . . but just what do children learn from their parents? And how do they learn it? The most recent research shows just how much even the youngest children learn from other people, and it's much more than we would ever have thought before. But the really striking result is that very little of that learning comes through conscious and deliberate teaching.

This book shares conscious and deliberate teaching, but also practices that can be done unconsciously. Modeling your values and creating norms and rituals are typically unconscious practices. You probably don't say, "I value family conversation. I'm going to develop a three-step plan for more conversation." Instead, you simply talk more as a family, or automatically turn off the TV or devices for that conversation.

Gopnik describes rituals as "actions that make little sense by themselves but serve important social functions. By performing very specific actions in a highly prescribed way, you can identify who you are or what group you belong to." Some examples of rituals may be how you eat, what you do first thing in the morning, or how you greet someone new. Gopnik continues, "Passing on rituals seems to be as important in cultural evolution as passing on technologies. In fact, you may argue that rituals are technologies. But they're social technologies instead of physical ones." Rituals can bind or divide us. In families, rituals can provide cohesiveness to the family. In the hustle and bustle of twenty-first-century life, a ritual like having breakfast together as a family can unite the family in a shared experience and be a protective factor against whatever the rest of the day decides to throw at you.

Gopnik describes an experiment that she conducted with young children in which they observed an adult perform a "complicated sequence of actions that had a sensible outcome, such as waving a pen in the air, twirling it around, and then putting it in the box." The children observed the behavior, then skipped the complicated twirling and put the pen directly in the box. When the experiment was tried again, the adult performed a more senseless action. "When the action seemed purposeless," Gopnik described in her book:

> When, for example, the experimenter took the pen off the table and then after twirling it elaborately put it right back in the same place, the children were much more likely to insist on reproducing every fine detail of the action themselves. When children imitate another's actions in this way they not only say I see how this works or I see that you know about this but also *I see that this is the kind of person you are.*

Rituals reinforce meaning and tell children who we are, our family's beliefs, our goals, and what we care about. If a family always has a television running in the background, that communicates a message. That creates a norm and a ritual. The ritual is "turn on the TV when you get home," and the value that communicates is "we are a family that cares about the TV." If a young child gets handed a phone when they are upset, the ritual is "handing over the phone," and the communicated value is "the phone can help you calm down." We may not intentionally mean to communicate these values, but we do, even if unconsciously and inadvertently, through ritualistic actions.

Consciously communicating healthy tech use at home can reinforce these values to your children and hopefully pass them on as they age and start their own homes. It is far easier to create a new norm or ritual with a young child than a teenager, although change can happen at any age. It's never too late to start something new or shift the way you think about technology at home. Think about your current digital parenting rituals. Do they reinforce your values? Do you enjoy them? Are they age appropriate? Have circumstances changed at home? Should you evaluate what you're doing?

Only you know the best technology rituals for your home, but here are some research-driven tech rituals to try:

- Do not use the phone as a self-soothing device for young children.
- Keep family mealtimes device-free.
- Only turn on the television to watch it, not as background noise.
- Commuting and driving with children (with the exception of long trips) are times for talking and singing, not using devices.
- Devices are turned off at a certain time of night.
- Children cannot play video games/watch TV until they finish their homework.

Over the last few years, I've trained hundreds of foster-care parents on online safety. Although the requirements can vary from state to state, most foster parents need a state license and a certain number of training hours on subjects such as first aid, mental health, the foster care system, child development, behavior management, and more. Among all of these subjects that foster parents must learn and handle, they also have to deal with technology in the home.

The 3 Ms of Fearless Digital Parenting is based on the concepts of model, manage, and monitor. But what happens when you are given a teen to foster and never had the opportunity to model or manage appropriate digital behavior? For example, one foster parent told me in a training that when they took in a ten-year-old, that child had absolutely no rules or norms about technology. The parent was at their wits' end and, frankly, tired. The expectations that this foster parent had around tech directly clashed with the (lack of) expectations in the previous home. This can cause conflict and battles in the home.

This conflict does not only occur with foster children, but also with any children who live in more than one household and have different sets of norms. It can be confusing for a child when things are allowed in one home, but not another. In an article about family routines and rituals published in the *Infants & Young Children* journal, the authors write, "Divorce has the potential to disrupt family life in grand form. Not infrequently, the households have different sets of rules about regular routines such as bedtime and mealtime behavior." In a study of 341 children of divorced parents, the article found that when bedtime routines were consistent, the children had better academic performance, fewer school absences, and better overall health. The article states,

(Continued on next page)

"children and adolescents raised in divorced households also reported fewer internalizing and externalizing symptoms when their custodial parent reported regular assignment of family roles and routines."

Divorced families or foster parents must work extra hard to model their technology norms and enforce any rules at home. While they may not have control over what happens with the other parent, or what happens in that parent's home, they can control what's going on in the here and now. This means a stricter adherence to routines, more reminding of rules, and keeping as many consistent parenting practices as possible.

Self-Regulation and Rules

A parent of a toddler may not want to hear this, but we need to teach our children to say no. Anne Collier, a youth advocate who runs NetFamilyNews.org describes the concept of *refusal*. "We need to teach our children how to refuse something that disturbs or overwhelms them. They need to know to turn it off, to walk away, or to go to Mom or Dad or a guardian to help them process what they've seen." Part of learning to do that is having our kids refuse *us*.

It's developmentally appropriate and normal for children to assert their boundaries with parents in the toddler and preschool years. That doesn't make it any less frustrating or annoying for us as parents, but self-regulation is a foundational skill that our children must learn. When children are nonverbal, like babies, that self-regulation may mean crying themselves to sleep. But when children are older, they can start expressing their inner boundaries and feelings.

With Digital Respons-Ability, we have a lesson aimed at elementary students on saying "no." We remind students that they are not necessarily "mean" or "giving up" when they say no. We also teach them different types of no's. Some of them include:

- "No, I need more time."
- "No, that's not safe."
- "No, I don't want to do that."
- "No, I need help."

Children need to recognize when they feel uncomfortable. Children also need to learn to refuse strangers, but it's more likely that a child will need to say "no" to a friend who wants to play video games when homework is not finished, or to an older cousin who wants to share something scary online. Children need practice in refusing and setting boundaries. Let them practice on you (despite your inner exasperation).

Creating Rules at Home

I recently had an exchange with my child about a hypothetical situation in which my army would invade his planet. Paraphrased, the dialogue went something like this:

Me: "If I were to invade your planet, I'd have to make sure I could live there and that there were supplies I want."
Him: "I have lots of things (he gives a list) and no one lives here but me."
Me: "Oh, I thought you had an army. It's just you there? Okay, then I'm definitely invading and taking over."
Him: "You can't. I control the planet."
Me: "Wait, how do you control the planet?"
Him: "I just do. I can do anything."
Me: "Okay. Well, I'll need to get other armies to destroy you."
Him: "Why would you destroy me?"
Me: "Well, you're basically all-powerful, I'd *have* to destroy you."
Him: "I'd destroy all your armies. Unless I was lonely in my swimming pool. Then you can come."
Me: "But if you let me come, I can't trust you not to destroy us. You might change your mind."

Him: "I wouldn't . . . maybe. But if I did, I'd bring you back."
Me: "Wait, you have power of both life and death?"
Him: "Yes. But I'd give you twenty chances to kill me."

This is just a snippet of what became a meandering conversation. It was also a frustrating conversation because the rules and story kept shifting. He blocked me at all attempts to rationally discuss how I would destroy the planet—he was all-powerful (and had a swimming pool, too!).

You may have had a conversation like this with your child. You're playing a game with them, but the rules change midway through. Or, if you win the game, they change the rules on you then. Young children view rules differently than adults. Rules are formed through cooperation and negotiation, not from an abstract authority figure.

In James Youniss's work, *Making Sense of Social Development*, the concept of children creating their own culture apart from parents is discussed. "By creating their own cultural system with peers, children establish a culture in which their own interests can be tended apart from the adult culture in which there are other interests operating, such as those specified by the school curriculum." This child's culture evolves into adolescent peer culture, which is even more segregated from adults. In this child culture, rules and boundaries are fluid and changing. Children make up the rules as they go, while adults see rules as fixed.

This differentiation between child culture and adult culture happens young. Research suggests that even at toddler ages, children form preferences with their playmates. By the time a child is in preschool, most have reciprocated friendships. A longitudinal study over two years that was published in *Child Study Journal* found that "children with at least one mutual friend at year one were better liked by peers a year later than children with no mutual friend."

Young children need friendships, and the space to form those friendships. Parents are and will continue to be an important part of their children's lives. But we are from a different culture, one with fixed rules, scheduled activities, and desired outcomes in the form of academic success. Young children do need fixed boundaries, but also flexibility. This is a quandary when developing norms and household rules. We need to be more like children when creating rules, and they need to learn more about adult culture by following them. The Internet makes this dilemma more fraught. Sometimes the consequences for breaking those rules online are severe, just as breaking the rule of "don't touch the stove" also has severe consequences.

When determining your rules for tech use in the home, separate them based on risk level and safety. In the stove example, we know that most of the time the stove won't burn us because it's not always on. Despite this, when we do break that rule, the consequence can be severe burns. What are the technology risks that have the most consequences? What will "burn" your child the most? And when looking at those risks, what are the most realistic ones?

Let's compare two potential online risks: cyberbullying and sex trafficking. Both of these topics are explored more in Chapter 6 on page 93, but for now, cyberbullying is generally far more likely to happen to a child than sex trafficking. This is because sex trafficking is rare and only happens on particular corners of the Internet, while cyberbullying is present on pretty much every online platform. While sex trafficking has a higher "burn" rate or consequence, it's extremely unlikely. Therefore, if you're creating rules based on fear of sex trafficking, it's like creating a rule in your home for young children not to remove the foundation vents in the house and crawl in them. Yes, technically they could try to find a way to do that, but they probably don't know what they are or how to get in them.

Focus on realistic rules of what young children might actually face online such as:

- Scary or disturbing content
- Curse words in videos and games
- Cyberbullying or people generally being unkind
- Sexual content like pornography

Those realistic rules also need to consider child culture and flexibility. The rules should shift as your child gets older. Managing online activities will eventually turn to monitoring activities from a distance. The Internet can be an amazing adult-free place where children can play, have their own rules, learn cooperation, make new friends, and learn. If we are so scared of the potential risks, small as they can be, we may create additional risks—having a child feel left out, lonely, or rejected by peers. It's the equivalent of being so concerned about a burn from the stove that we decide not to cook at home and order in unhealthy meals. Yes, no one will get burned, but there will still be consequences.

Screen Time

In the fall of 2019, my staff and I with Digital Respons-Ability trained over 500 parents on the 3 Ms of Digital Parenting in small groups around Utah. At these trainings, we surveyed parents on their biggest concerns about their children and technology. One of the top three issues among them all was "spending too much time on screens." Screen time is a frequent refrain I hear from parents,

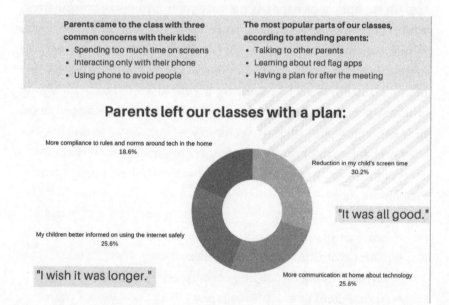

Parents came to the class with three common concerns with their kids:
- Spending too much time on screens
- Interacting only with their phone
- Using phone to avoid people

The most popular parts of our classes, according to attending parents:
- Talking to other parents
- Learning about red flag apps
- Having a plan for after the meeting

Parents left our classes with a plan:

More compliance to rules and norms around tech in the home
18.6%

Reduction in my child's screen time
30.2%

"It was all good."

My children better informed on using the internet safely
25.6%

"I wish it was longer."

More communication at home about technology
25.6%

educators, and sometimes even kids. Is my child watching too much TV? Are they socializing enough? Will being behind a screen affect their grades? Are they safe being on a screen so much? Years ago, I used to worry more about screen time. I read the media articles and my friends and I would express worries together. But after years of work in this space, reading, researching, and conducting my own surveys, I can safely say that screen time should not be a parent's biggest concern about their children's use of technology.

In April 2020, Jenny Radesky, a pediatrician and children and media expert, urged parents in *The New York Times* not to think about screen time in a negative way. "Even the phrase 'screen time' itself is problematic. It reduces the debate to a black and white issue, when the reality is much more nuanced." Part of the nuance in the screen time debate is lumping all screen time together. But not all screen time is created equal. What about online homework? Or playing games with friends? Spending time on screens with a family? Learning a new skill from YouTube? All of these activities are done behind screens, yet they have positive benefits. When we often do multiple things behind a screen or there is more than one screen, how do we even accurately account for that or truly measure "screen time"?

As mentioned in Chapter 2 on page 9, prevention science teaches us that human behavior is complicated and influenced by a variety of different individual, family, and community factors. But you wouldn't know that by the conversation around screen time. It gives the false impression that screen time is *the* reason why our child's behavior changes, but screens are an easy scapegoat and simple answer behind a host of different outcomes. We should look at screen time as a symptom of other underlying causes that can potentially make things worse. For example, if a child is already overweight, screen time could make their health worse by encouraging them to sit for long periods of time. But the screen time did not *cause* the weight gain.

Dr. Radesky suggests that we should approach screen time differently. "You know your child better than anyone else and are therefore the best person to decide what and how much media use is the right amount," Radesky said. She and others use the Three Cs framework: child, content, and context. These will be described more in Chapter 7 on page 133.

Screen Time and Young Children

When I teach the 3 Ms of Digital Parenting, I give parents the same advice I give myself—relax. But there's an exception for young children. Screen time for children aged eight and under should be more limited. Why?

- Children learn through modeling behavior and struggle to learn from screens.
- Children are learning language, and screens can interrupt with that natural development.
- Young children should be moving and active. They need to learn to crawl, walk, and explore the world.
- Sleep is important for every age, but particularly for young children as their brains develop. Screens can interrupt healthy sleep routines.
- Children need socialization. They are learning the rituals and rules of their family and the world. While screens can connect young children to family, they can also come between them and others.
- Children do not have the context to understand what they see and experience online. This can make them more vulnerable to predators and disturbing content.
- Children are learning to self-regulate, take turns, and calm their own emotions. A screen can be a distracting device that can impede that natural development.

Another reason to limit screen time for young children is: they may not even notice it's gone! I've seen my child have more fun with a stick or a box than any app. Little kids are masters at picking up whatever is around them and making it into a toy. They are on the move, tasting and touching all that the world has to offer. I remember getting my then-toddler one of those fake phones with the colorful buttons and sounds. He ignored it, preferring cardboard boxes. What benefit does a screen have for a young child who is perfectly happy with their toys and does not even grasp what they're missing?

Despite these facts, young children are on screens now more than ever. An analysis of young children's screen exposure published in *JAMA Pediatrics* found a large increase in screen time by children aged 0–2. From 1997 to 2014, screen time grew from 1.32 to 3 hours daily for infants and toddlers. While this study, based on diary entries over time, showed that screen time doubled by children aged 0–2, the researchers note that most of this screen time for young children is television. "As stakeholders warn against an overreliance on mobile devices," they write, "they should be mindful that young children spend most of their screen time watching television." According to this research, our infants and toddlers are watching close to 3 hours of television a day, 20 hours a week. Is that the best use of these young expanding brains?

Since that metanalysis in *JAMA*, the type of screen use by young children has shifted. More recently, Common Sense Media published a study surveying over 5,000 respondents from 2011 to 2020 on media use by children under age eight in the United States. They found roughly the same amount of screen media time over that nine-year period, but there was a switch from television viewing, the largest amount of screen use found in the 2014 study, to online video watching. The Common Sense Media report states, "For the first time, watching online videos on sites like YouTube now constitutes the largest proportion of children's total TV and video viewing, with an average of 39 minutes a day—more than double the amount of time devoted to online videos three years ago." After online videos, the next most popular form of media in this age group was streaming services. Overall, respondents to the surveys found that "more than a third of children age eight and younger watch online videos every day."

The American Academy of Pediatrics (AAP) published a screen time guideline in 2016 with recommendations for young children. The World Health Organization (WHO) has similar guidelines as the AAP, who encouraged parents not to give screens to children under eighteen months old. For children two to five years old, the AAP recommends limiting screen use to no more than one hour a day and says, "find other activities for your children to do that are healthy for their bodies and minds."

Clear-cut guidance by the AAP stops when children enter school. This is where things get more nuanced and complicated. There are no specific hours they recommend but they do say to limit media use on mobile devices. Why this limit specifically on mobile devices? Think about when you're on your phone. Are you sitting next to someone? Are you talking to someone while you text? Probably not. Mobile devices like tablets and smartphones are isolating. Growing children who are learning to read, write, and talk need to socialize with others.

COVID-19 may upend the screen-time debate. Because people are stuck at home taking virtual classes, working from home, and doing online homework, etc., we are *all* behind a screen more. As the aftermath of the pandemic continues, we may need to update our research and look at this issue a different way. I am very curious to see what any parents in the years to come have to say about screen time. I suspect that they may have other tech concerns on their mind.

Distracted Parenting

Life is busy. Adults are more connected than ever. This connection comes at a cost, however. For those in the service economy, work doesn't necessarily stop at a certain time of the day. You are always reachable and texts, calls, emails, and notifications can come at any hour of the day. This is a stark contrast to how you may have grown up. Perhaps there was a phone or two in the home, a landline. Maybe it even had a cord. If work called that phone, it was an emergency. There was more of a separation between work and home. The COVID-19 pandemic has blurred those lines even further. Work *is* at home. The living room or kitchen also serves as an office. There are few clear boundaries between the personal and professional. Caregivers are especially busy.

A confluence of technological, economic, and other changes have made parents and caregivers more connected, and more stressed. While the idea of workplace burnout is not new, it's been given increased attention during COVID-19 as remote and virtual work gets blended into the everyday. The American Psychological Association reports that half of parents of children in mid-2020 said that their stress levels were high and that managing their kids' online learning was a significant source of their stress.

When parents are stressed, this can have an effect on their children if they deal with their stress by retreating into TV binges, games, or online scrolling. A thesis from the University of Nevada in Las Vegas (UNLV) in 2018 interviewed and studied parents' smartphone use. After talking to parents, they found that "one of the most common themes reported by participants was a concern and desire for connection." Parents would use the smartphone to connect, even though they expressed that their communications online lacked depth. Other participants "reported that using a smartphone left them feeling less connected or missing the deep connection afforded via face-to-face interaction." This smartphone use, in a desire to connect, actually disconnected them from their children.

Another finding from the UNLV study was that some of the parents used the smartphone not only to connect, but to disconnect and destress. One of the parent participants said in an interview, "I think I've seen parents get on phones to shut down from dealing with kids. Like, it's kinda become a trend and coping mechanism in a way." This finding is ironic because one of the top three concerns parents expressed about their kids in my parenting surveys was that they were "using their phone to avoid people." Parents complain about their children using the phone to disengage or to connect, while they are often doing the same thing.

To clarify, it's understandable to want a break. Life is busy. I do it myself sometimes; the bathroom with its locked door can be a brief respite and time to scroll and just breathe. But it can also be important to take a step back and look at our own behaviors. We are both connected and disengaged, distracted by the demands of work and home. Technology expert Linda Stone coined the term "continuous partial attention," and this parental interaction style has real harm.

As young children develop, they learn words, language, and the norms and rules of the world through modeling and watching their parents. Infants and toddlers in particular learn through a "serve and return" type of communication. For example, when an infant babbles, the adult may look at the infant's face and say, "Oh, yes! I agree," or smile with enthusiasm. This encourages the infant to babble again; they love the attention they get from caregivers. This helps with early literacy. Infants who have this interactive style know about twice as many words at age two than other children.

A phone comes in between these dyadic "serve and return" exchanges. It interrupts the process. Instead of eye contact and a direct response, a parent who's working on a laptop may simply grunt, "uh huh." Parents are sending a message, although not intentionally, that the computer or smartphone is more important than their child. Over time, chronic inattention can stop a young child from bids for attention. The child realizes that they aren't going to get their parent's eye, so why even try?

Neglect can have severe lifetime consequences. Researchers who studied the tragic situation of infants in Romanian orphanages in the 1980s found that the severe neglect in those early years (no toys, no touching, and being in cribs all day) had lasting effects. As these children grew, they were found to have poor impulse control, problems with regulating emotions, low academic achievement, and more.

Occasional inattention is fine. Your children do need their own space and lives too, just as you do. But when it chronically happens day after day from when they are infants to when they reach school, it can have lasting and hurtful effects. What's even worse is that smartphones and work calls are unpredictable. Notifications can happen at any time. This can confuse the child. One day the parent is attentive and listening, the next they ignore them. Parents are both present and not available emotionally.

Parents should not just look at their child's device use, but their own. Here are some questions parents should ask themselves:

- Do I need to be on my phone right now?
- Can I leave my device in another room?
- Can I answer this call/email/message after my child goes to bed?
- What are my own device-free times/zones of the house?
- Am I modeling good tech behavior for my child?

Suggestions for Parents

AAP's media use guidelines recommend that parents "co-view or co-play with your children." I suspect that some parents reading this may inwardly groan. I get it, young children's taste in media can be stiflingly dull. I remember my son's love of *Pokémon* and the television show's rote, silly, and routine episodes. In *Pokémon*, the adults are portrayed as buffoons and the ten-year-old protagonist, Ash, wanders around the world with only his backpack and other kids. I kept thinking, *where are his parents?* Despite my lack of love for *Pokémon*, it was a way for my child and me to bond. I would listen when he talked about the show and we played on the *Pokémon Go* app together, which not only got us moving, it was fun too.

What are some ways you can have screen time with young children aged 2–5?

- **Watch shows with them.** This doesn't mean that you need to be glued to the screen next to them, but if a show is in the background, comment on it. Ask what the child thinks of a certain character or plot. Ask your child what they think will happen next.
- **Use screen time to encourage play.** If your child has a favorite show or character, you can use this to get them out from behind the screen. When my child was a toddler and in preschool, he, like many other children, loved the show *Thomas & Friends*. From this love we got a wooden train set that not only encouraged learning and play, but interested him more than the show.
- **Use screen time to get active.** There are games and shows that get children moving. For example, the *Pokémon Go* app gets you out walking and catching Pokémon.

I understand the fears behind screen time. The hours have definitely increased, particularly with young children. But it doesn't have to be scary, it can be a bonding and learning experience. Yes, be vigilant and stricter for young children, but overall, we can all collectively take a deep breath. There are plenty of things to fear out in the world, screen time doesn't have to be one of them.

For young children, caregivers are modeling, whether intentionally or inadvertently, the norms and values they hold dear. You are teaching your child outside the classroom with your actions, words, attention, and examples. "Parents matter. Children learn from their parents and other caregivers, whether they are learning by observation or learning through testimony. They look carefully at what parents do and listen just as carefully to what they say," wrote child development researcher Alison Gopnik.

This chapter advised specific actions and words to help you digitally parent. This is important, but the basics of love, attention, and consistency are just as important. Gopnik writes, "fundamental relationships of trust are more important than teaching strategies." At these young ages, parents can create that foundation of trust, love, and caring that can extend as children explore, grow, and experience the real and online world.

Chapter 4
The Second M: Manage
(Ages 8–13)

THIS chapter is personal to me. As I write this, my own child has joined this cohort—not a little kid anymore, but not yet a tween. At eight he is already very tall, and I know that puberty is just around the next birthday. He is both snuggly and independent, knowledge-able and ignorant. It can be an unsteadying feeling as a parent, these children-but-not-quite-children that change so fast. I'm sure I'm not the only parent to think privately when looking at their child, *Weren't you a baby, like, yesterday?*

To parents, the infant years were not long ago, and toddlerhood seems closer than adolescence. Kids these ages also feel unsteady, although from their perspectives they are long gone from toddler-hood. Their bodies are growing, and they wake up differently than the day before, literally. Hormones are released through the body overnight. Girls typically start their periods while they sleep. Kids go to sleep as children and wake up as adolescents.

Children start puberty somewhere between ages eight and four-teen, girls sooner than boys. Puberty is different for each child, and they may feel differently about it. Boys who develop sooner have higher confidence of their strengthening and growing bodies. Boys who develop later may be bullied about their appearance and feel left out in athletic activities. Girls can also be bullied from puberty. They may feel insecure about their developing breasts and height. Girls who look older may have different expectations and treatment from their peers and the adults around them.

I experienced this personally with my height and appearance. I am about six feet tall and reached that height at age sixteen. I towered over my peers in middle school, dropping my confidence. I wanted to hide. I remember vividly the experience in eighth grade when our entire class lined up from tallest to shortest for the annual class picture. I had to walk past hundreds of students to take my place as the second tallest person in the grade. At that age when I was desperate to fit in, walking past the entire grade felt like a walk of shame. In those tween years, I would frequently hunch over so I wouldn't be seen, which did little to hide my light blonde hair and fair skin. Other girls would tease me about that, calling me "Powder" after the 1995 movie about an albino. In fifth grade, a group of the "popular" girls in school approached me in gym glass and told me I needed a bra, looking at me with disgust. In middle school, I was also told disdainfully by an older girl that I needed to shave my legs. My earlier development was a source of fear and shame, not pride.

Every child experiences puberty, but in general, puberty can be harder on girls. Claire Shipman and Katty Kay, authors of *The Confidence Code for Girls*, write in the *Atlantic* on the significant drop in confidence when puberty hits.

In our research, we worked with Ypulse, a polling firm that focuses on tweens and teens, to survey more than 1,300 girls from the ages of 8 to 18 and their parents. The girls surveyed were asked to rate their confidence on a scale of 0 to 10, and from the ages of 8 to 14, the average of girls' responses fell from approximately 8.5 to 6—a drop-off of 30 percent. Until the age of 12, there was virtually no difference in confidence between boys and girls. But, because of the drop-off girls experienced during puberty, by the age of 14 the average girl was far less confident than the average boy. Many boys, the survey suggested, do experience some hits to their confidence entering their teens, but nothing like what girls experience.

Why this confidence gap? Psychologists and researchers believe that girls ruminate and think extensively on feelings, often negative ones. Girls are often more likely to people-please the adults around them. As children turn into adults, there is more need for risks, and this lack of confidence causes girls to risk less. School rewards girls for listening and staying still, but the workplace does not offer the same rewards for being quiet.

Fearless digital parents should reflect on the question of whether they are raising fearless daughters. Are you encouraging and praising your daughter for taking risks? Do you have different expectations from your daughters than sons? Puberty is a time of a huge confidence drop for girls, and you can help mitigate that drop.

In addition to hormones, changing of appearance, and other social and emotional developments, this is also the age where children typically get their first smartphone. Between these ages they begin creating their digital identities and navigate that space unassisted. According to the 2019 Common Sense Media Census, more than half of all children have a smartphone by age eleven. By the time they are teenagers, about three-quarters of them own a smartphone. The cute cohort of eight-year-olds who haven't started puberty and likely haven't had a phone turns quickly into a gaggle of sexually developed thirteen-year-olds, all with access to the Internet in their pockets.

Growing Independence

A desire to do things on their own, pursue individual interests, and follow curiosities are some of the markers of this stage in development. Children are developing agency and seeing themselves as separate from their parents and caregivers. They may see technology as a means to get that agency and separation. Caroline Knorr, the senior parenting editor at Common Sense Media, describes the entrance to this new developmental stage:

> Around 7–8 is the age of reason; that's when a child is able to determine that what they're seeing isn't necessarily reality. They themselves realize they have some agency, and their parents aren't the center of the world. They start to notice you in social situations, [and] start saying, "Why did you do that?" They notice that they are separate from you.

I've seen this in my own son through the game Minecraft. He has created elaborate worlds of blocks, secret hideouts, underground caves, farms, ships that are his (and only his), etc. He will sometimes share these worlds, but often he likes to have his own space and keep his online world to himself. When I ask him about his creations, depending on his mood he will either eagerly answer questions or give one-word responses. This can be hard as a parent, when we're used to our kids talking constantly and hanging on our every word. For younger children, parents can be the center of their world. They are the best models, their heroes, their friends. Over time, parents move away from being the center of their world and may find themselves in another galaxy altogether.

The Internet can show children that larger world and give them opportunities to explore those interests. It can also show them a more frightening and uncertain world. They learn that the choices they make online have consequences. And that people outside their orbit do not always mean well.

Peer Influence

Friends are hugely influential for older kids and tweens. According to an article published in *Developmental Psychology*, peer influence peaks during these years. Ages 10–14 are the height of peer influence across a person's lifespan. Children are looking to their peers on what they should be saying, wearing, eating, watching, and doing. These older children start asking questions like, "Why is this like this?" and comparing friends. "My friend Javier says this, but Dad says this." They see more differences between friends, and begin to question beliefs, values, norms.

Recently, my son was disciplined by a teacher for using certain words. He was unfamiliar with what the word meant and didn't know it was a "bad word." He just knew it was something some classmates used. He was upset to be disciplined and probably confused when I tried to explain the nuanced concept of certain words, that they could mean different things, and there were certain places you should say certain words, and other places you shouldn't. Reflecting now, I realize that the whole experience must have been bewildering—with different people having different rules at different times in different places. But he's at the age where those differences are making more sense than before.

When your child was younger, you may have been able to maintain a simple technology rule such as, "Only twenty minutes of playing time on your tablet after dinner." Now, children are capable of more complex and changing rules such as:

- "You can be on your tablet all day in this class."
- "You can't be on your tablet during this other class."
- "You can be on your tablet longer doing homework."
- "You can't be on your tablet after this time of day."

- "On the weekends, you can be on your tablet after this time of day."
- "If you're at your aunt's house, you can't be on your tablet at all."
- "If you're at Grandma's house, you can be on a tablet all you like."
- "You can play this game on your tablet, but not this other game."

Of course, the important things about rules are consistency and communication. While the rules may be varied, they should be enforced. It's only a suggestion, not a rule, if it doesn't have consequences. At this age, there can be more gray rules, not just black and white. Moreover, you can help make up some of the rules *with* your child instead of *at* your child. You can also get some honest feedback from them about the rule.

Rules can be a battleground for tweens and teens. They are observing different rules in their peers. One friend may be allowed to have a smartphone or play a certain game. They may question you on why—and probably use that phrase every parent has heard at least once: "It's not fair."

Here are some suggested tech rules to use with children aged 8–13:
- Parents must know passwords of any social media accounts their children have.
- No online purchases without permission.
- Devices must be turned in at night before bedtime.
- No tech time at least an hour before bed.
- Let parents know who your friends are online.
- No sharing of personal information to people online.
- Parents will assist on signing up for any online accounts.
- If finishing homework online, only one tab is open at a time.

This is why I share a Golden Rule of Rules in my digital parenting classes:

Be the mean parent.

Now, when I say the word "mean," I don't refer to belittling, yelling, or cruelty. Mean is not a behavior, but a label. Stick that label proudly on your shirt: I am a mean parent. You are the unfair parent. You are the parent that sticks to that myriad of rules. You are the parent whose child complains about your rules. You are the parent who stands firm when told, "You're so mean. My friends all have one!" You are the mean parent.

Why do you care what your ten-year-old's friends think? You are not in the age range of 10–14 developmentally. At your age, the idea of worrying about what your friends think may be laughable. You do not follow fashion trends or what's "hot." You care little about the most popular shows and only watch what brings you joy. You are unfashionable, uncool, and your presence brings forth eye-rolls. You are not your child's friend. You are the mean parent.

Your child, on the other hand, cares deeply about appearances. They want to fit in. They want to have friends. They are keenly aware of what's going on around them. They will remember decades later being told by a pack of fifth-grade girls to wear a bra. Their experiences, heightened by the hormones of puberty, etch deeply in their memories and feelings. They are more fragile. They don't have the life experiences to know that "this is not the end of the world" and "it will get better." They need you to be the mean parent. They need you to be the scapegoat.

Understand at these ages how important peers are. Doubtless you haven't forgotten fully; you may still remember a mortifying incident at age twelve, a bullying, a teasing, a feeling of being left out. Reflect on those feelings, dulled by time, and try to empathize with your child. Take on the eye-rolling, the arguments, and be firm. If you have a rule about no phones, let your child blame you. It is so difficult for children to stand up to their peers at this age because of where their brains and bodies are. While we should encourage them to resist peer pressure and set boundaries, we should also understand that it's much harder than we think. If they can blame you for tech rules, they save face. When they respond, "My mom is so mean; she won't let me on Instagram," they will be greeted with an, "Oh, yeah, my mom's awful too," not a prepubescent judgment of coolness or fitness to be a friend.

As they move out of the Manage phase into the Monitor phase, you'll need to be less firm on these rules. But for now, as they're navigating these tricky waters of social hierarchies, peer pressure, puberty, and technology—stick to those rules. And let your child blame you.

First Phone

The battle of mean parents versus peer-influenced preadolescents often comes to a head around the issue of getting a phone. When children enter the Manage phase at age eight, only a small percentage—around 20 percent—own a smartphone, according to a 2019 Common Sense Media report. By the time they exit that phase at age thirteen, the majority have their own phone: about 72 percent. This has changed rapidly; as recently as 2015, the majority of tweens never had their own phone. But now, in a few short years, your child will look around their classes to see more and more of their peers getting a shiny new phone.

When parents are confronted with the inevitable question, "When can I have a phone?" parents should respond, "What do you need a phone for?" It's a question all families should ask, and they may come up with different answers. In families where parents share custody and children move back and forth between households, a phone can be a necessity. In other families, children are involved in lots of out-of-school activities where they may be at different places in the evenings and weekends, and that can necessitate a phone. Other older tweens may babysit their siblings and need a phone for emergencies. There are numerous reasons to get a phone earlier than later. There is not one magical age or answer.

Consider alternative solutions, such as the parent or caregiver being a go-between. Offer to share your phone for them to call a friend. One father of a ten-year-old I interviewed hooked up a landline and told his children that they could share this number with their friends. However, that landline did not get used because their friends didn't have phones. This is often the case at those ages; unlike teens who mostly do have their own phones, there is a wide discrepancy between ownership in the 8–12 age range.

As kids in this range get older, you may find that having parents act as the middleman becomes a barrier to communication. At younger ages, like 8–11, the alternative solution of the parent go-between can work. But when children enter puberty, they become highly aware of how they look to others and having to be the kid who says, "Can I have my mom text you?" may limit their communication and embarrass them with friends. After age eleven, as the rate of phone ownership starts accelerating, kids who rely on their parents to act as middlemen can end up feeling left out of peer groups and activities. While you do want to stick to rules and be the "mean parent," you also have to understand that peers are crucial for your child's development. They need to be able to talk to their friends outside of school. Because there is no hard-and-fast age when it's "best" for a child to get a phone, you may need to continually evaluate the situation, taking into consideration a variety of factors.

Here are some questions and prompts to give your child when they start asking about a phone:

- Why do you need a phone?
- What friends of yours have a phone?
- Can you use Mom/Dad/Grandma's phone for now?
- How would you use a phone?
- What makes you most excited about a phone?

Let them articulate their reasoning—they may surprise you. And while the answer, "Because all my friends have a phone" may be frustrating, it's a valid response. To them, all their friends having a phone is a very important reason to have one. But dive into that response more. "How does it make you feel that all your friends have a phone?" "Why do all your friends have a phone?" Whatever your answers are, none of them should be, "because I said so." Your child is growing and getting a better understanding of the world and differences. Explain to them your decisions.

You can make me, the author of a book on tech use, the mean parent. Cite an expert to your child. You can make a pediatrician or psychologist the mean parent. Give your reasoning, whether it be safety or concern about them having time to participate in hobbies and finish homework. Express to your child with love your concerns about their safety. Don't express fears with panic and hyperbole but with love and care.

What *do* the experts say on smartphone ownership? One expert, Dr. Sarah Coyne, recommends "start slow instead of giving full access to everything. Practice, whether it's on a flip phone or a phone with a lot of restrictions." Your child should demonstrate that they can be responsible on a phone before there's more access and fewer restrictions. Coyne has had struggles with phone ownership in her own home. "I have a twelve-year-old right now, she just lost her phone. She had this junkie flip phone laying around the house. I wanted her to show me she was responsible around it." Coyne ended up getting her a new phone but had her daughter pay half of the cost. Her other older son "went through four phones and I said, 'I'm done with your cell phone plan and paying for your phones.' Eventually he figured it out after he started to pay." Coyne established consequences from her children's actions, which all parents should think about before giving their children a phone. What will you do when the phone gets lost or damaged? Who is ultimately responsible for the phone?

The question of when to get the first phone is one that I'm frequently asked when teaching digital parenting classes. While I stand by the notion that there is no single "right" age for smartphone ownership, based on the research I find a strong argument to be made to delay smartphone ownership until later in the Manage phase, until 12–13 or so. The reasons include strong peer influence; it's a distraction; children struggle with self-regulation; and online safety. But again, I hesitate about a very black and white and firm answer on this subject. Every family and child are different. There are valid reasons for having a phone during the tween ages.

When you're considering getting your child's first phone, you must also consider social media. To a tween, a phone equals social media in many cases. Dr. Coyne describes the developmental stage these tweens experience. "This is a tricky stage. A lot of them will get on social media for the first time. They're going through puberty, peers are really, really important. They're distancing from parents and making those attachments to friends, which is developmentally appropriate."

The intense influence of peers is part of the argument to delay the first smartphone. They are getting closer to peers and socially comparing themselves to others. Social media can exacerbate those sometimes-negative feelings of social comparisons. "Their identity is often based on comparisons with peers," said Coyne.

I like to compare getting a smartphone to riding a bike. You put training wheels and extra support on the bike the first time you ride. As time passes and you get more skilled at riding, the training wheels come off. Ages 8–11 are a time for training wheels; or not riding at all and using a scooter. But if your child needs a bike to get places and it's inhibiting friendships and their life, it's better to get one with training wheels than not at all.

Here are some ways to encourage communication and practice with communication devices before giving your child a fully Internet-enabled phone:

- **Hook up a messenger or communication app on an existing tablet.** If your child has a tablet, use that tablet for them to communicate instead of a phone. Facebook, WhatsApp, or other accounts can be used on the tablet where it's easier for parents to monitor. This gives tweens opportunities to talk with their friends, but with the understanding that parents may see the conversations.

- **Get a dumb phone.** You don't have to get an Internet-enabled phone; there are other options. You may remember the old Nokia phones from your teen years: they're back. They only send texts and make calls. You can also find older phones on eBay or other sites.
- **Get a smartwatch.** For children who are walking far to school and need a way to contact parents, a smartwatch is an option. For example, Vtech offers the Kidizoom, which has some phone features like games and photos. This market continues to grow and there are many other options.
- **Strip down an existing phone.** This is a method for younger children, not older ones. I knew of a parent who stripped down their iPhone for their fourteen-year-old; the teen took the phone back into the store and got all the privileges brought back. There are many YouTube videos out there to bypass restrictions as well. But for younger children, this can be an option. On the iPhone, restrictions can be set up for Internet access. Parental controls can be set on Google Play and the Apple Store to block downloads. Data usage can be restricted. Apps can also be uninstalled on Android and iPhone devices (although sometimes the app remains in internal or external memory). Parental controls will be discussed in more depth in a later chapter.

Whatever you decide for your family on smartphone ownership, communicate and talk it through. See the Appendix on page 209 for more help on questions to ask about your child's first phone.

Online Safety for Children in the Manage Years

While it may be difficult to think of, children are rapidly becoming sexual creatures. Their bodies are developing, hormones are flowing, and they are thinking about sex. This time of self-discovery is an ideal opportunity to have open conversations and share the facts and details. Go to a Planned Parenthood puberty class, check out books, share factual videos, and educate children. Hundreds of studies have shown that sex education can delay sex until older ages, increase contraception use, prevent pregnancy, and more. The topic of sex will continue in a later chapter, but for these ages, smart digital parenting also means recognizing that children going through puberty have sexual desires and curiosities.

Children are picking up from parents, educators, and others around them that the Internet is full of sex. That's not "wrong" per se; there is a lot of sex online. But there's sex in other places, too. You probably watched "sexy" shows or movies when you were young. Sex has always been part of media. And there's lots more to the Internet besides sex.

We want our children to understand that there are both negative and positive consequences to having a smartphone, and that they have both the ability and responsibility to control what content they consume—and what content they put out into the world. Caroline Knorr explains:

> It's really important to talk to tweens about their own personal responsibility and accountability on navigating their own experience. We want to make sure that kids are sharing appropriately. If they're putting something out there that is sexual and provocative, people can get the wrong impression and that can invite predatory behavior.

Knowing that young people are highly concerned about what their peers think, parents can encourage better communication and sharing online. These conversations may feel uncomfortable, but by allowing your child to process some of the Internet's sexual or confusing content with you better equips them to stay safe online and make good decisions when you're not guiding their every move. Ask your child questions such as:

- What do you think your friends would think about you sharing that?
- When you see a post like that, what do you think?
- What kind of message do you think that person is trying to send?
- How do you feel when you see something like that?

Caroline Knorr uses the word "Red Flag Feelings" to describe those uncomfortable/creepy feelings that tweens may feel when interacting and communicating online. Parents should encourage their teens to act on those gut instincts, those red flag feelings.

Young children should be taught to identify emotions; that's the first step. Children in the 8–13 age range should not only be taught to identify how they are feeling but also to reflect upon those feelings. Help your child learn to:

1. **Identify the feeling.**
2. **Reflect upon the feeling.** Why do I feel this way? Have I felt this way before? What does this feeling mean to me? Are there multiple feelings I'm having?
3. **Act.** Talk to a trusted adult or friend. Flag the post or report the incident. Step away from the device.

Gut instincts are often correct, and we should help our children recognize and act upon those instincts.

At these ages, children are often imitating. They're desiring to fit in, but don't always know the context of all the social situations, memes, images, jokes, and more. Parents should not assume that if a child made a sexual joke, their child really understood the joke. Children will make jokes, or use "bad words" to fit in, not necessarily because they are rebelling or trying to cause trouble. Assume the best intent or assume ignorance. When you respond with calmness and compassion, your child will be more likely to share with you in the future. If you immediately react punitively, it's more likely that your child will hide the jokes or memes and you lose an opportunity for a trust-building discussion.

Along with assuming the best about your child, make your relationship a safe place for them. As children grow past the Manage phase into the Monitor phase, they will need that safety and trust even more. This is the time to make sure your children know that they can come to you with anything. Trust takes a long time to build, but a short time to destroy. Build up that trust more and more through these years as they have their training wheels on.

Once they get on that bike, kids want to ride. That can be frightening. I remember when my child was three and got his first push bike. There was a hill near our house that he wanted to ride down, and I vividly recall seeing his body wobble and almost tip the whole way. I held my breath though; I knew that if I shouted out and expressed my own fears he might look back and lose his focus. But I also knew he had a helmet, the bike was close to the ground, and there was grass below. I had placed some guardrails and given him instructions; then I had to sit back and let him experience bike riding.

I need to give my child space online, just like I did with his push bike. I admit, I am afraid when I think of my eight-year-old potentially being in exploitative situations online. But if I react with fear and shame, he won't talk to me if it happens. I must not only be the mean parent and set my rules, but I must also be the calm parent. I must not make the problems about me, and I must remind him that he's loved no matter what. It's an unsteadying age, and there will be wobbles, which means that parents need to be prepared to stand even more firm.

Chapter 5
The Third M: Monitor (Ages 13-18)

IN the early and adolescent years, the brain is saying "get up and move!" Because of this, I half-joke that, developmentally, teenagers are "less cute toddlers." There's some truth to that. Like toddlers, teens are rapidly changing. Your teen's time of intense change is occurring at a time of intense technological change. They're moving away from parents into both real-life and digital spaces where their caregivers can't reach.

It's not easy for parents. I've heard parents describe living with teens like "being on a tight rope" or "walking on eggshells." You're trying to balance their need for autonomy in a changing, shifting, and sometimes dangerous world. Author and leader in cognitive science Dr. Alison Gopnik sums up adolescence and this balancing act:

Adolescence, like early childhood, seems designed to be a period of innovation and change. The difference is that the agenda is no longer exploring the world in the safe context of a protected childhood. Instead, your job as an adolescent is to leave that protected context and actually make things happen yourself. The profoundly paradoxical job of the parents of teenagers is to allow and even encourage that shift to happen.

As a parent you spend years ferociously shielding your children from risk. But when they become teenagers you have to figure out how to turn them into independent people who can take risks themselves.

I use the word "monitor" to describe this hands-off approach. While the word "monitor," to some, implies spying, I describe it like a parent on the other side of the room who is fixing dinner but listening. You're watching, but rarely intervening. You're communicating, but not interrupting. This chapter will discuss monitoring strategies and share perspectives from teenagers on the topics of sex, mental health, social media, and more.

Physical Changes in Teens

In the book *Adolescent Development and the Biology of Puberty*, it states that "Adolescence is one of the most fascinating and complex transitions in the life span. Its breathtaking pace of growth and change is second only to that of infancy." Toddlers and teens are very alike. A toddler has emotional ups and downs and throws fits; a teen has emotional ups and downs and, while they may not throw themselves on the ground crying, they have their own fits. Both groups have growth spurts. Adolescent girls typically reach their full height around age seventeen, and boys at nineteen. Toddler tantrums usually stop around age three as they move to the next stage of development. In teens, most dramatic changes of puberty like periods, pubic hair, hormonal changes, and more finish around age fourteen.

Those dramatic changes are preparing teens for their next stage of development: sexual maturity and adulthood. "Research conducted with both humans and nonhuman primates suggests that adolescence is a time for carrying out crucial developmental tasks: becoming physically and sexually mature, acquiring skills needed to carry out adult roles, gaining increased autonomy from parents, and realigning social ties with members of both the same and opposite gender," claims *Adolescent Development and the Biology of Puberty*.

Other physical changes include:

- Eating more
- Stronger sexual desires
- Ability to communicate like adults
- Gaining more muscle, particularly in boys
- Larger breasts in girls and testes in boys
- Hair on the face in boys
- Voices continue to deepen in boys
- More acne in both genders

These changes are not linear and coordinated. Bodies and brains develop at different paces. For a teen, their prefrontal cortex, which is responsible for decision-making and long-term planning, develops in their early twenties when they are sexually mature. This disconnect between brain and body is a reason for caregiver vigilance. Teens are lacking some of the brakes in their brain when making risky decisions. They're sexually mature before they're cognitively mature.

Sexual Education
Sex in the digital world can skew perspectives and beliefs on what sex is actually like in the real world. Bodies are carefully curated. Acrobatic acts create performances but not pleasure. And messages about gender roles, consent, and norms are distorted. Sex education and caregiver communication can debunk myths, protect against pregnancy and sexually transmitted diseases (STDs), and prepare teens for healthy relationships. Unfortunately, both types of communication can be limited, banned, or incomplete. Peggy Orenstein, author of *Boys & Sex: Young Men on Hookups, Love, Porn, Consent, and Navigating the New Masculinity*, writes about sex education:

Until young people—girls as well as boys—are better educated about gender socialization, sexual consent, ethical engagement, mature relationships, and diverse orientations, we will be stuck in damage control mode. Such lessons ought to be actively integrated into school curricula, taught in, though also beyond, human development courses (which we colloquially, if too narrowly, call "sex education"); instilling basic values of citizenship is, after all, part of the job of educational institutions. Yet, realistically, only twenty-four states and the District of Columbia currently mandate sex education, and only ten require that it be medically accurate.

Sex ed is often taught in a single class period or assembly and its focus is more on pregnancy and STD prevention, not how to have healthy, consensual relationships. The type of sex education that teenagers are most likely to get is abstinence-only. The US federal government has invested over two billion dollars in abstinence-only sex ed. Despite all this money, metanalyses of these programs' lessons "have been found to neither significantly delay intercourse compared to others nor have fewer partners," said Orenstein. However, these programs have often led to "higher rates of pregnancy and STDs. Equally concerning, while pleasure-based sexuality education that includes practicing refusal skills has been found to reduce rates of assault, abstinence-only programs have not."

Why are abstinence-only programs less effective? It relates to prevention science and the *why* of behaviors. Teenagers are rapidly becoming sexually mature and there are biological factors encouraging them to have sex. Simply saying "nope, not gonna have sex" isn't going to rewire the brain. Other reasons teenagers have sex are because they are in relationships. The desire for sexual intimacy is healthy and trying to repress those desires is extremely difficult. Peers, family, and the media also play a role in adolescent sexual behavior. There are biological, peer, social, relationship, and media pressures to engage in sexual activity.

Abstinence-only education does not give tools and skills to deal with these pressures. It simply focuses on the bad but does not touch on how sex can be a bonding and pleasurable activity. It's the equivalent of someone only talking about how the Internet is full of misinformation and porn. That statement is true, albeit a generalization. The Internet does have a preponderance of fake news and porn, but it also has reliable news and ethical and sensual pornography. We need to communicate to adolescents with more nuance, noting both the positives and potential negatives.

Talking to young people about sex can be nerve-racking. *What if I can't answer their questions? What if they ask questions about* my *sexual activities? By asking, am I encouraging them to have sex?* One of those fears can be put to rest. "Decades of research have made it clear that talking to children about sex does not reduce the age at which they start," writes Orenstein. "Our teens are in urgent need of high-quality human development courses. Until those exist, relying on school sex education is a risky bet. And that means unless caring adults step up—parents, physicians, youth advocates, faith leaders, coaches—the default educator will be the media."

How do you talk to your teen about sex? Here are a few suggestions:

1. **Pick a neutral and casual location.** Bring up sex in the car or during some physical activity. If there is a scene in a movie that you're both watching or a news report comes on related to sex, bring up your questions in a low-key manner. Calling your child into your room at a predetermined date is like being called into the principal's office. It may make them defensive or nervous.

2. **Talk often.** One stat mentioned by Orenstein is that the average length of a sex talk is just ten minutes. If your child only got a ten-minute talk in their lives, they will definitely be lacking information. Talk about sex habitually, and briefly. Have many ten-minute conversations, not just one.

3. **Talk about consent.** Let them know that consent for sex needs to be obtained in person and asked directly. Consent is also crucial for digital images. If they receive a nude photo,

they should not forward or post it without the permission of the person in the picture.

4. **Sex is more than intercourse.** Talk about oral, anal, and other varieties of sex. There is more to sex than a penis entering a vagina. STDs can be spread through other sex acts, and those acts need consent as well.

Here are some conversation starters you can try with your teen:

- How does technology affect dating relationships? What do you see?
- What pressures do you think guys and girls feel in different dating situations?
- What does coercion or pressure look like to you?
- What does consent look like to you?

Boys get unhealthy messages from porn, the Internet, and their peers on masculinity, what relationships look like, and sex. These messages can affect their future relationships, muddy the waters of consent, and leave them feeling lonely. Journalist Peggy Orenstein writes:

> Mothers and fathers (and any other adults in a guy's life) need to challenge the unwritten rules of male socialization, the forging of masculinity through unexamined entitlement, emotional suppression, aggression, and hostility toward the feminine. Close relationships, whether platonic or romantic, have been found to be the number one key to personal well-being, and emotional literacy.

Boys need their caregivers and adults in their lives to provide a different story. Encourage your son to identify and express his emotions. Both boys and girls can be affected by the conditioning and conversations online and with peers. They need to know that there are different ways to behave and think. "Boys too then need a strong counternarrative to develop grounded, realistic perspectives on women, men, sex and love. Frankly, without it, there is a chance that they won't see women as fully human, and that they will view sex as something a female partner does *for* them, and that they do *to* her."

Healthy Online Relationships for Teens

If we have concerns about our children getting involved in nonconsensual sexting and online sextortion, we should teach them about healthy relationships. The model of prevention science has us look behind the screen at the why, so why do these behaviors occur?

Consider this case study based on a real-life scenario. A freshman girl is in her first dating relationship. She is excited and feels very mature. But that excitement changes to apprehension after a few months into her relationship when she is pressured by her boyfriend to share graphic and nude images with him. She cares about this boyfriend and wants to stay with him. Since this is her first relationship she doesn't know if his request is "normal" and she feels uncomfortable talking to others about it. She just knows that she feels uncomfortable and wants to refuse, but also wants to be a "good" girlfriend and stay together.

Teenagers are starting their first dating and romantic relationships in these years. This is new, exhilarating, and sometimes confusing. Unlike their parents, they have little context for what a healthy relationship looks like. *How much should I see my girlfriend? Where can we touch each other? Are we exclusive in this relationship or should we see other people? Should I even call him my boyfriend?* There's no manual for this, and teens may have never had a discussion with parents, mentors, or educators on dating relationships.

I was the same age as the girl in this case study when I got my first "official" boyfriend. Except my idea of official was different than his. Both in middle and high school there seemed to be these "rules" for what girlfriends and boyfriends did. You were supposed to hold hands in the hall, but not kiss. You were supposed to sit together at lunch and call regularly after school. You were supposed to go on dates. I brought those hidden rules into my first relationship, not knowing any better. But he had a different set of rules from his experience, and we had different ideas of what the relationship looked like which, ultimately, led it to end.

Technology has created more unwritten rules of relationships. There may be one "rule" that contradicts another. You should broadcast your relationship on social media, but not brag. You should text every morning and night, or is that too much? Your partner should not be following any other girls' feeds, or maybe they should, and you shouldn't be so jealous? Girlfriends should share sexy photos with their boyfriends, or not? Porn is not allowed, or should it be? It can be confusing for adults, let alone teens.

When one feels uncomfortable with a request or the action of their partner, they should speak up. "Rules" should not dictate a relationship. "Rules" should not coerce someone into behaviors that they would not normally participate in. "Rules" can change and shift depending on the environment, cultural context, and generation.

Teens are hugely concerned with their peers' opinions, a subject that will be discussed later on in this chapter. This concern can make them follow their peers' rules, which may have no basis in healthy relationships or norms. For example, if a teen boy hears other boys talking about their sexual activities, he may think that's normal and a "rule" and join in even if he doesn't want to.

Parents need to talk about healthy relationships not through rules, but concepts. And more than just talk, parents should demonstrate those concepts through their own romantic relationships. When a young person grows up in a home with fighting, passive aggressive behaviors, lack of communication, or abuse, they may believe those behaviors are "normal." When you're talking to an adolescent about healthy relationships, it's a good time to take stock of what you're modeling to them.

Some concepts that determine healthy relationships are described by Planned Parenthood, who offers healthy relationship classes and other resources for adolescents around the country. They describe these concepts as pieces of a solid relationship:

Respect
- Are you proud of each other?
- Do you listen to each other?

Trust
- Do you feel secure in the relationship?
- Can you spend time apart from each other and feel okay?

Honesty
- Can you admit when you're wrong?
- Can you talk openly about your feelings, even when it's hard?

Equality
- Do you both compromise?
- Do you both get to make decisions about your relationship?

Communication
- Do you talk about your feelings with each other?
- Can you disagree about something without disrespecting each other?

Along with pointing out healthy aspects of a relationship, parents and caregivers should also share unhealthy aspects. Media can be a tool for this conversation. You can mention healthy or unhealthy relationships in a TV show or movie that you're watching together to teach these differences in a casual and nonconfrontational way.

Planned Parenthood describes what an unhealthy relationship looks like:

> Lying, cheating, and disrespect are signs of an unhealthy relationship. So is trying to control your boyfriend/girlfriend, even if it's out of jealousy and even if they say they do it because they love you. Controlling behavior includes things like checking the other person's phone without permission, keeping track of everything they do on social media, or telling them who they can or can't hang out with.

Technology serves as a tool of greater communication, but also a tool of greater control. When a partner tries to get a person to sext, tracks them on accounts, requires them to text them regularly, or forbids them from talking to others online, they are trying to control the other. Teens who are unfamiliar with what relationships look like may confuse that control with love or caring. Parents should monitor their teens that are in dating relationships for potential red flags.

Some other technology-related red flags include:

- Demanding passwords or other login information from their partner.
- Catfishing behavior (their partner pretending to be someone they're not).
- Hacking into accounts.
- Expecting immediate responses over text or phone.
- Accusing of cheating or not caring about them if their partner does not respond fast enough, send sexts, or do what they say.

These red flag behaviors occur not because of technology itself but because of insecurity and other internal issues of the person exhibiting this behavior. Technology is a tool for them to get that validation and their needs met. If parents encounter any of these red flags in their children's relationships, they should tread carefully. If someone is controlling and abusive, they will try to drive a wedge between their partner's other relationships, including their parents. Parents who come down very strictly may offer more ammunition to the boyfriend or girlfriend who is demonizing and separating their partner from their loved ones.

Unfortunately, teen dating violence is too common. According to LoveisRespect.org, funded through the US Department of Health and Human Services, "One in three adolescents in the US is a victim of emotional, physical, or sexual abuse from a dating partner, a figure that far exceeds other types of youth violence." If a parent does suspect abuse, LoveisRespect.org offers some tips:

- Listen and give support.
- Accept what your child is telling you.
- Show concern.
- Talk about the behaviors, not the person.
- Avoid ultimatums.
- Decide on next steps together.

Having a healthy relationship with a loved one is a protective factor against many risky behaviors. But an unhealthy relationship can contribute to trauma, mental health issues, and more. I've heard the saying from other parents: your children give you both the greatest joy, but also the greatest pain. Being in a relationship makes you vulnerable and can hurt but is also part of having a fulfilled life. Teenagers are learning about relationships and these lessons can affect their entire lives. Parents can be a mentor, a safe space, an example, and a teacher on healthy relationships, which will help their children both digitally and in the real world.

Teen Mental Health and Online Behavior

Understanding why teens do what they do online means understanding their brains and biology. They are adults sexually, but not emotionally. They are like adults in strength and fitness, but not in reason. These proto-adults need understanding, patience, monitoring . . . and sleep.

Teenagers and Sleep

Teenagers are often characterized by adults as moody and angsty, and yes, they do have hormonal spikes at these ages, but a big reason for their moods is lack of sleep. Their brains are going through spurts of activity, and those brains need a rest. The National Sleep Foundation reports that "teens need about 8 to 10 hours of sleep to function best. Most teens do not get enough sleep—one study found that only 15 percent reported sleeping 8½ hours on school nights."

Teens try to catch up on their sleep on the weekends, but this can create a bigger problem. Irregular sleep patterns are connected to mental health concerns. The body has its own internal clock, or circadian rhythm, and it doesn't like to stray far from its schedule. Human development researcher Dr. Sarah Coyne said, "right around puberty circadian rhythms shift about 2 hours later." That means a ten-year-old who was asleep by 8:30 p.m. may be a twelve-year-old who falls asleep by 10:30 p.m.

Unfortunately for teens, there are two big obstacles standing in the way of decent sleep: school and screens. Adolescents are living in a world created by adults, who do not sleep the same way. More researchers and parents are becoming aware of these obstacles. There have been national calls for districts to start high school later. Research supports this policy change, although logistically it can be difficult.

Starting in the 2016 school year, Seattle moved their middle and high school start times to almost an hour later. When researchers at the University of Washington studied the results before and after the change, they found "students got 34 minutes more sleep on average with the later school start time." The researchers found improvement in grades and reduction in absences and tardiness. Teachers at the school reported that the students were more engaged in discussions and their work. Interestingly, moving school time later did not result in teens staying up later. The lead researcher Gideon Dunster reported "we've put them in between a rock and a hard place where their biology to go to bed later fights with societal expectations."

Other expectations of teens relate to screens. Their homework and friends are online. Teens need to get more sleep because school starts early, but they also need to get on a computer to finish their homework. Adolescents are often busy in the afternoons with sports, clubs and more, so homework may not start until late. Sometimes they will *have* to be on a screen at night. In addition, this evening time may be one of the only periods of the day away from parents and rules and the only time to talk with friends. Unfortunately, the sometimes-necessity of screens has few simple solutions. Teens are in between a rock of homework and early start times, and a hard place of biological and social needs.

Screens interrupt sleep through the emission of blue light. That's the light we see in the sky that tells our body it's time to wake up. But screens also interrupt sleep because of activities, conversations, information, and other fun that may be much more appealing than going to bed. A metanalysis of adolescents between 2002 and 2014 published in the *International Journal of Health Policy and Management* found that teens on screens more than two hours a day "had 20 percent higher odds of reporting sleep-onset difficulties. The strength of the association between screen time and sleep-onset difficulties increased over time, which may reflect a change in the type of screen time use (e.g., the increased use of easily accessible screens such as smartphones and tablets)." Since the data collection began in 2002, there are exponentially more mobile devices, and more ways for teens to stay up at night with screens.

No wonder teens are moody. They're forced to obey rules they didn't create that their bodies rebel against. This puts parents in a tough spot. Sleep is vitally important, but so is graduating high school. This may lead to conflict between parents and their teens. But there are some things parents can do to monitor and better regulate technology to improve their teen's sleep.

- **No phones in the bedroom.** Even if a phone is in the room with notifications turned off, the awareness that there *might* be a notification can impact sleep.
- **Charge the phone in another room.** If a phone is charging in the same room as your teen, even several feet away, it can still be a distraction with lights and noise. A solution to this is having the phone charge somewhere else. If your teen struggles to follow phone rules at night, charge the phone in your room.
- **Use sound machines and alarm clocks.** A sound machine can produce white noise, which is the combination of many noises that mask other sounds. There are some alarm clocks and smartphone devices that can set white noise along with alarms. Try not to use your cell phone for an alarm, just buy a simple alarm clock.
- **Turn off notifications and turn on sleep mode.** Utilize the sleep or night mode setting on the phone to keep it still. Turn off notifications except for phone calls. Use the Do Not Disturb function to limit calls to certain contacts.
- **Utilize night mode/night shift and dark mode.** Night mode/shift is a setting on the phone that changes the colors of the displayer to warmer tones. Dark mode inverts the color scheme from light backgrounds with dark text, to dark backgrounds with white texts. More social media, like Facebook, now offers a dark mode. In addition to saving battery life, it can limit the amount of blue light emitted through the phone.
- **Use timers and shut-down apps.** There are different apps and timers that parents can set at night. Use parental controls to adjust settings or shut down your Wi-Fi at night.

- **Have a tech cutoff in the evening.** Try to enforce at least thirty minutes of no technology before sleep. An hour or even two is better to help your body wind down.
- **Read on a book, not a tablet.** The book *Why We Sleep (Unlocking the Power of Sleep and Dreams)* by Matthew Walker reports that "compared to reading a printed book, reading on an iPad suppresses melatonin release by over 50 percent at night. Indeed, iPad reading delayed the rise of melatonin by up to three hours, relative to the natural rise in these same individuals when reading a printed book."
- **Evaluate your own sleep habits.** If you have norms around sleep in your home, are you demonstrating them to your teen? You will have little success getting your teen to sleep if you are also staying up late on devices.

Risks and Rewards

When I was a youth services librarian, I was introduced by teens in my library to Slender Man. This character, originally created on the forum Something Awful, and meme-ified and mythologized across the Internet, found a new home in a video game: Slender: The Eight Pages. Slender Man is exactly how he's described, a tall, no-faced being in a black suit that has an eerie presence. For a month in 2012, the teens could talk little else but Slender Man and the game. In this survival game, you walk through dark forests and buildings trying to collect eight notes, with droning and mysterious noises in the background. While you navigate this scenery, you must avoid the Slender Man, who may suddenly pop up and end the game.

As an adult, I found the game terrifying, and the meme silly. I just didn't get it. Why did these teens keep subjecting themselves to this creepy game? They would complain about how scary it was yet play again. It became a noise issue in the library because they would scream and disturb other patrons. In my opinion, there were many other free and better-made games online, why did they insist on playing this one over and over?

Part of the answer to that question involves the teen brain and how it reacts to risks and rewards. Neuroscientist B. J. Casey writes that adolescence is the developmental period "when an individual is probably stronger, of higher reasoning capacity, and more resistant to disease than ever before, yet when mortality rates increase by 200 percent. These untimely deaths are not due to disease but to preventable deaths associated with adolescents putting themselves in harm's way." The teens playing Slender were engaged in somewhat risky behavior, but in a safe environment. They not only got a burst of adrenaline from playing, but they had the opportunity to show off to their peers how "brave" they were for playing. Perhaps, in some ways, we adults should be grateful that there are scary games, movies, and other media for teens to safely engage in risky behaviors. They are physically safer outlets than drugs, fast cars, or stunts.

Another activity that the teens in my library would do, less safe than Slender, is jump off the wall that surrounded the side of the building. A few teens even injured themselves from trying to take a big leap off the side. Time and time again I would remind them not to  jump off the wall, but they would still do it. I found myself only giving those reminders not to jump when there was a group of them. A lone teen would simply sit on the wall, but one teen in a group would often attempt the jump.

Just like teens are primed to seek risk, they are also wanting rewards. And one of the biggest rewards for a teen is a social reward. Playing a scary game in front of peers, or jumping off a wall, is a way to get one type of social reward: attention. We see this attention-seeking behavior from teens online regularly. Perhaps it's an Instagram post at the gym, or a provocative Snap, or sharing a controversial and polarizing opinion—all are ways for teens to get social rewards. When adults look at these teenage behaviors and shame them, saying "why would they post a picture looking like that?" or "why do they believe in such nonsense?" we're kind of missing the point. Teens may not always prefer to dress or act or say certain things. Their motivations are based on the opinions of others, not their own. Me telling a teen not to jump off a wall could conversely add to the problem. *Now* when a teen jumps off the wall, after an adult tells them not to, the act has even more risk and a greater reward.

This goes back to a theme of this book, the why. It's hard as adults to put ourselves in an adolescent's shoes, because that adolescent has a different brain. B. J. Casey explains that these reckless risks "are in part due to diminished self-control—the ability to inhibit inappropriate desires, emotions, and actions in favor of appropriate ones." The prefrontal cortex of teens is not fully developed. It's hard for them to forecast the future, make plans, and be patient. Of course, technology is wonderful for those who lack self-control, there are stimuli in every nook and cranny of the Internet.

It can be a struggle parenting an individual who is creative, active, and with near-adult intelligence—but lacking impulse control. Parents should give their child space to take those risks because they can provide rewards, whether social, intellectual, or emotional. While, yes, there are risks from the Internet, compare them to bigger risks outside. Driving is inherently less safe than browsing the web, and we don't think twice about doing it. We adults may roll our eyes or look in confusion at certain games or apps, but we should consider them from a broader perspective. Are they really so dangerous?

Also, consider the world now. There are fewer public spaces than before. Our neighborhoods are more scattered, and you need a car to get just about anywhere. As a librarian, I saw this firsthand. The library was one of the few places that teens could hang out (mostly) away from adults. Teens may be using social media and gaming because there's no other way to get away from their parents and other adults. It's a space just for them where they can create their own rules, not rules imposed on them. The scholar danah boyd spent thousands of hours with teenagers observing how they used technology. She found that social media was often used to distance themselves from parents, to experiment, take risks, and establish a community. Teens have always distanced themselves from parents. That's normal. What's new is the medium.

I've also spent thousands of hours with teens, and I can say first-hand that what boyd reports is correct. Unlike what the media may report or parents fear, teens are mostly goofing off and hanging out online. It's just a digital version of them strolling around the park or mall or in earlier centuries going down to the village square. Like the park or mall or village, there are risks, but the rewards of community and connection can outweigh those risks.

Social Media and Teens

A group of teens were interviewed in the spring of 2020 about their relationship with technology. They spoke frankly about social media and its impacts. Sylvia, a high school junior, shared "I have mixed emotions about social media because it's a good way to find inspiration if you are doing crafts or whatever. But then there is a lot of jealousy in wanting to be somebody else because their body is this way, and they have this stuff."

Ramos, a high school senior, echoed Sylvia's mixed feelings:

I agree a lot with Sylvia in that social media has a unique power for both good and bad. I think social media inspires a lot of really good things. It helps GoFundMe pages to go viral so that people can get the support that they need. There are so many other ways that social media can be transformative and good, but there are also a lot of ways in which people internalize the things that they see. This goes for things like body image, but also for people of color not seeing people who look like them having influential roles in social media, in film, and other places. Seeing white beauty being valorized forces them to internalize the notion that they are different and unvalued and unworthy of being on social media or being shown off like that.

Like Ramos said, social media has a power for good or bad. And while one may cut back, block, or refuse to use social media, it can impact our lives. To be clear, however, those impacts are not solely caused by social media. Prevention science teaches us that behavior is a potential outcome from a variety of different individual, family, and community factors. It is misleading to state that social media causes mental health issues. Social media is more a symptom than a cause.

A 2020 study published by Dr. Sarah Coyne looked at over 500 adolescents over a period of eight years to examine the connection between social media and mental health. The report stated, "Many studies have found a link between time spent using social media and mental health issues, such as depression and anxiety. However, the existing research is plagued by cross-sectional research and lacks analytic techniques examining individual change over time." This basically means that the existing research about the effects of social media on adolescents only takes a snapshot of their behavior. We've all had bad days, and on those bad days a post might bother us more than other times. A teen could report a different result on a day when they got little sleep or fought with a friend. Their feelings about social media change depending on what else is going on in their lives.

The study goes on to say, "Results revealed that increased time spent on social media was not associated with mental health issues." Mental health issues, like the stressful, happy, or confusing things that happen to you a particular day, are preexisting. Look at social media like a mirror to one's mental state. In addition, it can exacerbate preexisting mental health concerns. If you are depressed and scrolling through your feed and not interacting with people, well, that can make you feel more depressed. Social media also has the power for good, and a depressed person can connect with others or participate in an activity that lifts their mood.

When we at Digital Respons-Ability survey teens in digital citizenship classes about their social media usage, they report different opinions than the current fear-based media narrative reports. We asked approximately 3,000 teenagers in the fall of 2019, "Does social media make you feel better about yourself?" and "Does social media make you feel worse about yourself?" About three times more teens said yes, it makes me feel better, than no. Like Sylvia and Ramos, however, many teens had mixed feelings. Fifteen percent of the surveyed teens answered that social media "maybe" makes them better, or maybe worse. This is a highly individual question, and a teen may answer it differently depending on their life circumstances, or just how they're feeling that particular day. But it's helpful for parents and caregivers to see that in general, most teens see positives with social media, and it does not always affect them negatively.

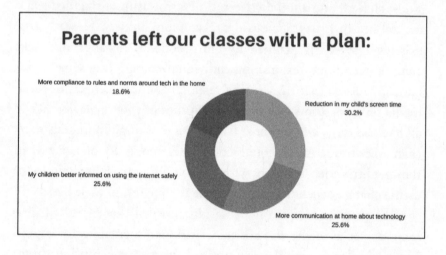

Social Comparison

We are wired to socially compare, says Dr. Sarah Coyne. "Social comparison is evolutionary-based . . . saying 'don't compare' is not realistic." In Coyne's research on the topics of adolescents, technology, and social comparison, she found that one potential negative of social media is that it puts us face-to-face with unattainable looks, material things, and lives. "Research suggests that photo-based social media sites are worse for social comparisons." These photo sites use heavy editing, filters, and more to present an unrealistic idea of reality.

Sam, a high school senior, describes their feelings on social media.

> There are definitely good and bad pieces to it because sometimes it will make me laugh or I will see things and I will be like good or cool or funny. But a lot of times it does make me feel bad about myself seeing other people and their lives and how good their lives seem on social media. I'm sure that is not how it is in real life but a lot of people's lives on social media are portrayed as perfect and a lot of people will have perfect bodies, or what society says is a perfect body. And sometimes it can make me feel insecure and not good enough. There are definitely good and bad pieces to it. It's hard, with social media, to have one without the other. You get both, which sucks.

Parents are at a different developmental stage than adolescents. They've had more time with their own bodies and brains, and those bodies may be a comfortable fit. I remember as a teen feeling much more concerned about my looks. Acne made me cake on makeup and braces made me hide my smile. But as I've aged, I've become more comfortable with my curves and, yes, still the occasional pimple. For me, Coyne's advice makes intuitive sense. Of course, you shouldn't compare! But while it may feel right to me, it's not right to say to a teen. Just like statements such as "don't bully others" or "get over it, it's not that bad" or "you should never ever look at porn, it's bad" aren't very helpful.

Coyne describes a way for parents to teach their children about social comparison in ways that *are* helpful: to communicate about media and ask empathetic questions. If a parent sees a picture of a girl that may be reflecting unrealistic beauty standards, they should "stop and say, 'okay, what's the backstory here? What makes her cry? What makes her struggle?'" Coyne says to "humanize that person instead of objectify that person and then we're less likely to have a negative experience." There's always a human behind the screen.

Teens are on Snapchat. The digital marketing firm Zephoria said that "As of April 2020, Snapchat reached 90 percent of all 13–24-year-olds." While there has been some progress by Snapchat to appeal to the 25 and up crowd, the vast majority of users are younger. It's a space for teenagers.

While there have been many news reports about Snapchat and sexting (and, yes, sexting definitely happens on Snapchat), it's typically not used that way by teens. High school student Ramos described his use of the app: "Snapchat is the main way I communicate with most of my friends." He adds a comment that may make parents feel aged: "Facebook is too old and most people our age don't generally interact on it." Another teen, Sylvia, added: "My brother is twenty-one and all his friends use Facebook and so do a lot of people around his age. But I have never had people around me use Facebook. Which I find very interesting because that is his main form of social media. And for me it's like Instagram and Snapchat even though I don't post that much on Instagram."

Teens see Snapchat as texting. They may in fact text less and Snap more. An average Snapchatter opens their app thirty times a day. High school student Sam described how he and many of his peers use Snapchat: "Snapchat is probably my main way of communication with my friends. I don't really know why, but that is usually how we talk, instead of texting or anything. I really like to use that just to keep in touch with people and talk to my friends."

What Teens Want You to Know about Social Media

The teens interviewed for this chapter were asked what they wished their parents and caregivers knew about their social media use. Writing as an "old" person who uses Facebook, I will bow out and give you their thoughts. We old people can definitely do a better job of listening to the teens in our lives.

Emory, high school senior: "I think my parents are too concerned about technology. Especially when it comes to YouTube and email. When something doesn't go as planned or if I'm not sleeping well, they will usually blame it on my use of technology. I try to tell them that maybe I'm just having sleeping problems because I'm a teenager and not because I'm on my phone. I feel like they are too concerned about phones instead of other things."

Ramos, high school senior: "The first thing that comes to mind is when I have done something wrong, and their immediate reaction is 'because I'm on social media too much.' That's probably a common misconception, but it is indicative of a broader distrust of social media. And I can only speak to my parents, and they were not okay with certain apps, and they were strict, and that's good to a certain degree. Their reaction was just a symptom of their paranoia of it. Overall, their regulating my time on social media was good, but there was a degree to which it was not okay."

Sam, high school senior: "I wish they knew that I'm not addicted to it because I actually don't go on social media that much. It's not the first thing I go to when I have nothing to do. I feel like whenever I'm sitting with my mom, and I get a Snapchat notification or if I open up Instagram for a second, she always says, 'Oh you are so addicted to social media.' And that kind of bothers me because I am really not at all. I know a lot of people who like to go on it more, which is totally fine, but that's just not me, and I think a lot of parents think that their kids are addicted to social media when that's not always the case."

Sylvia, high school junior: "I think it is similar to what Sam said. Sometimes if they see me on social media, they assume that is the only thing I do. And then they give me a lecture about how they didn't have a phone back when they were my age and didn't get one until they were way older than me."

Lupita, high school senior: "What I would like my parents to know about social media is that a lot of times it can be a news source. It gives me information about the world. I don't often watch the news, but that doesn't mean I can't get it in a different format. Also, that there are a lot of communities on social media and it is a good way to find people who share your interests, or personalities, so it is a good way to meet people."

Chloe, high school senior: "My mom is on Instagram and Facebook so there is a lot of stuff she already knows. But if there is one thing that I want to tell her, I would have to rewind the clock and tell her to make sure you know what your kids are looking at, just because there are some things that I have seen where I have been like I wish I hadn't seen it. I wish I could just tell my parents what I have seen to make sure that my younger sister isn't subjected to the same things. Social media can be an awesome resource and a great place to meet people, but it can also hold things that are crazy and awful."

Both parents and their teens have a complicated relationship with social media. It can amplify, calm, connect, or isolate. While different generations use social media in varying ways, there is still overlap and common ground. There are also misunderstandings. A first step is going in without any assumptions and being open to communication and other opinions and ideas. It is important to understand that social media, particularly Snapchat, can just be a communication tool, not a space for predators and dangers. Striking a balance between protective parenting and stepping back to monitor and observe can help you as a parent realize that technology is a tool and just one of many factors in your teen's life.

Red Flag Behaviors

What *should* parents be concerned about? Look at behaviors, particularly radical departures from normal routines, interests, and moods. It can be difficult to know what your teen is doing behind a screen. Platforms are password protected, moderated, messages disappear, and private servers keep out prying eyes. The next chapter covers some of those red flag platforms and apps. Yes, you'll want to monitor apps and tech use, but more importantly, you'll want to monitor behavior.

As mentioned earlier, monitoring shouldn't be like Big Brother. It's more hands off. Look at monitoring behavior as a security system in the background of your home. You're probably not aware of the system most of the time, but it's doing its job. The security system should not alert you of every little thing. *A strange dog got close to the house! The neighbors across the street are having a party!* If your security system went off on every little thing, eventually you'd ignore it—or get rid of it entirely. Likewise, if you go to your teen with every single concern, your teen will ignore you or get very defensive. Security systems, like parents with maturing teens, should only step in when there's serious concern. Teens need the opportunity to resolve some of these online issues themselves.

It's difficult to know when to step in. It's something I'm dealing with personally with my child. He experienced some bullying earlier this year and part of me wanted to question him on all the details and rush to his day care demanding "What's going on?" The other part of me, the less emotional one, wanted him to see this as an opportunity to communicate, talk to his teachers, and handle the situation himself. I went with the logical part and talked to him about what happened, but mainly checked in with him and the day care. I didn't push and I didn't make a scene. He later became friends with the bully, although one week they get along and the next week they don't. Sometimes I question my decision, particularly with their up-and-down relationship. *Do I say something to my kid? Do I try to talk to the other child's caregiver? Do I talk to the teacher?* I don't always know the answer. But I do know these things: he still wants to go to daycare, he has friends there, and there's been no serious physical or emotional injuries.

Parenting is making judgment calls without always knowing all the information. We're a megahertz processor trying to interpret terabytes of information. We can only observe and monitor signs, words, and behaviors, and try to find the best solution with that limited data. The black screens of devices can mask even more of that information. But we can look at the individual with the screen for signals, red flags that something is up.

Some red flag behaviors include:

- Increased media consumption that goes along with less time spent on hobbies and activities your teen used to enjoy.
- Dramatic changes in diet and eating habits.
- Grades dropping.
- Excessive sensitivity to any type of criticism or feedback.
- Repeatedly refusing to join the family at designated family times.
- Anger and/or tantrums when devices are taken away.
- Very secretive about online use, very secretive.
- Abandonment of their friends.
- Wanting to access credit cards or money regularly for online activities.
- Tiredness and moodiness.

Some of these red flags may simply be changes in bodies and sleep cycles. Teens are also beginning to date and developing their own identities with pressures and influences from peers, the media, school, and more. Adolescents, because of their developing brains, are at a higher risk for unhealthy and dangerous behaviors. This means your early warning security system should be vigilant. However, parents should mainly monitor and mentor, not ban and berate. As Dr. Gopnik said, "As a parent you spend years ferociously shielding your children from risk. But when they become teenagers you have to figure out how to turn them into independent people who can take risks themselves."

This hard task as a parent of teens means monitoring and encouraging self-efficacy. Teens need to have the confidence that they can resolve their own problems and accomplish their own tasks. This means not always rushing to the school asking, "What's going on?" but gently checking in at home for your teen to tell you what happened, and then doing more listening than lecturing. If you continue to do that—to listen without judgment, provide safety and security with little intervention—one day they will be the ones checking in with you.

Chapter 6
Online Safety

WHEN you picked up this book, this may have been the first chapter you opened. Online safety and dangers certainly get a lot of attention. When I bring up these topics in my digital parenting classes, that's when the parents lean forward in their seats. I joke that I'm the "boring" instructor on digital parenting because, while I do address online dangers, it's more peripheral to my main points: developmental stages and practical strategies for digital parenting. There are other lecturers on this topic that jump straight to the juicy stuff, packing auditoriums, and I admit the scary headlines and titillating sexual topics get attention. But I see both my and my staff's role not to scare parents, but to educate them. What good would it do just to recount the horrors and headlines? How would that help?

Consider this analogy. Let's say you wanted to know more about snakes. There are over 3,500 snake species in the world, but only 600 are venomous. Snakebites are a problem and kill thousands of people in the world. However, most deaths are from just four species concentrated in South Asia. So, if I were to lecture on snakes, I could spend an hour or two describing the consequences of snakebites (i.e., "untreated black mama bites kill everyone," "a Russell's viper has the most painful bite of all venomous snakes and will make your skin necrotic).

That would certainly be an interesting presentation. I could show you pictures of snakebites, charts of deaths, and even bring in a live snake that would hiss as I talk. But how helpful would that be? You probably don't live in South Asia, and if you did, you would have access to antivenom treatments. You would certainly be more knowledgeable about snakebites after my lecture, but would that help you avoid them? You would remember my presentation, though. The fear that coursed through your body when viewing a necrotic appendage would stay in your brain. However, you wouldn't leave with a greater understanding of how to actually prevent snakebites. You may leave my snake lecture even more terrified of all snakes, and unable to differentiate between the majority which are harmless versus the ones that can hurt you.

Snakes can be compared to the Internet. Yes, you can get "bit," but most areas online are not a problem. However, if I'm afraid of the few "venomous" parts of the Internet, I may assume all sites are bad. My fear may drive me to black-and-white thinking, generalizing, and impulsive reactions. A good snake presentation would not only talk about bites, but also talk about how to identify the venomous versus normal snakes. For example, some helpful knowledge would be how to differentiate between a coral snake (venomous) and its look-alike, a scarlet king snake (harmless). A good digital parenting presentation, or book, would not just talk about online dangers, but also talk about online opportunities.

This chapter discusses very real online dangers. But keep in mind, as you read, to put them in context. Understand that they are just part of the Internet, and that just like with a snake, some good protective gear and training can help keep you and your family safe.

Cyberbullying

Cyberbullying is a big topic in the world of online safety. But how often does it actually occur? Dr. Justin Patchin is a professor of criminal justice at the University of Wisconsin-Eau Claire and the codirector of the Cyberbullying Research Institute. He has surveyed and tracked cyberbullying in the United States and other countries for years. In 2019, he aggregated his data tracking cyberbullying from over 25,000 middle- and high-school students in the United States.

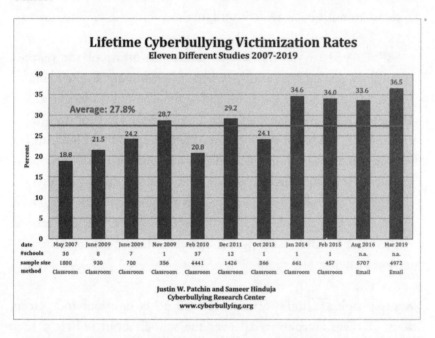

Lifetime Cyberbullying Victimization Rates
Eleven Different Studies 2007-2019

Average: 27.8%

date	May 2007	June 2009	June 2009	Nov 2009	Feb 2010	Dec 2011	Oct 2013	Jan 2014	Feb 2015	Aug 2016	Mar 2019
#schools	30	8	7	1	37	12	1	1	1	n.a.	n.a.
sample size	1800	930	700	356	4441	1426	366	661	457	5707	4972
method	Classroom	Classroom	Classroom	Classroom	Classroom	Classroom	Classroom	Classroom	Classroom	Email	Email

Percent values: 18.8, 21.5, 24.2, 28.7, 20.8, 29.2, 24.1, 34.6, 34.0, 33.6, 36.5

Justin W. Patchin and Sameer Hinduja
Cyberbullying Research Center
www.cyberbullying.org

Patchin and his coresearcher Dr. Sameer Hinduja found varying rates of cyberbullying since 2007 and note an increase in reports over the last five years or so. But overall, about 28 percent of middle and high school students since 2007 have been a victim of cyberbullying. In addition, about 6 percent of students admit to cyberbullying others, although this may be a lower number than in actuality because students may not want to admit it.

Twenty-eight percent is not a low number, but it's certainly not a majority. However, from media reports and attention, one may assume that this number is much higher. Students and educators may assume this too. Before I really researched the statistics, I thought the number was higher. In my conversations with students, cyberbullying was a hot topic, and they had opinions they wanted to share. But perceptions do not mean reality.

Anne Collier, a tech writer and youth advocate, encourages telling "kids the truth about bullying, the actual statistics, and the social norms researchers talk about." She goes on to describe a study at a middle school in New Jersey that shared positive perceptions of their students to push back against bullying.

> When you survey the school at the beginning of the year of kids' perceptions and how bad cyberbullying is, then you find that it's not as bad as kids thought. You put posters up all over schools like "83% of kids in our school are good to one another." Behavior conforms to that perception and bullying goes down even more. We need to tell kids the truth and get them facts. We need to be clear about what bullying is, anyways—it involves some sort of power imbalance whether it's emotional, psychological, or physical. It's repeated and targeted aggression. Two people arguing, that's called conflict, not bullying.

Young people are highly attuned to their peers' opinions and perceptions. If there are posters all over the school about bullying, their friends are talking about bullying, and the media covers it, they are going to think cyberbullying is everywhere and they are the next victim. Collier states that cyberbullying is a possibility, "it is the most common online risk kids face." However, it may not be as much of a risk as students, parents, and educators assume.

Cyberbullying Risk Factors

If parents and school administrators want to prevent cyberbullying, they should not assume it's lurking everywhere, or that every child will fall victim. A better approach is looking at it through the lens of prevention science, with risk factors. Some children are more at risk for cyberbullying than others, and more attention and education should be focused on that group.

A review of research around violence, cyberbullying, and traditional bullying helps us narrow down the risk factors and protective factors which can help prevent cyberbullying:

Risk Factor	Protective Factor
Lack of empathy	Ability to feel empathy toward others
Mental illness	Access to mental health treatments
Lack of coping skills when dealing with losses like a breakup	Effective coping skills
Unsupervised and unrestricted access to the Internet	Afterschool programs and/or pro-social activities to fill up unsupervised hours
Boredom	Hobbies, activities with peers
Lack of sleep	Strict bedtimes at home, later school start times, no technology in the bedroom, medical interventions
Victim of cyberbullying	Support from others and quick response by authority figures against cyberbullying
Member of a marginalized community	Accepting community environment

The risk factors on this list are focused mostly on the individual. However, many risk factors like poverty, racism, and sexism are systemic. Behaviors and choices are not made in a vacuum, but in a society. These societal and historical problems will not go away easily. As long as there are people and peer groups, there will be exclusionary behaviors and bullying. But just because the risk factors are large and long-standing, does not mean prevention cannot happen. Prevention science engages multi-tiered strategies involving caregivers, individuals, and systems.

Parents should look beyond the home to the school, peer groups, and other outside influences when addressing cyberbullying. The problems may be originating from platforms and people that parents do not know about or have little control over. But parents do have control over some areas. They can:

- Make sure their child gets enough sleep.
- Keep their child engaged in unsupervised hours.
- Know who their child's friends are.
- Provide them with resources for their mental health.
- Quickly respond if cyberbullying occurs.
- Educate them on healthy relationships and coping skills.

Types of Cyberbullying

Under the dark umbrella of "bullying" there are different motivations and intents. Understanding the "why" of someone's behavior won't alleviate the hurt, but it can change how you react to it. Knowing someone's backstory or motivations does not provide an excuse, but an explanation.

Here is a chart that summarizes some major types of cyberbullying:

Type of cyberbullying	What is it?	Where does it typically occur?	Potential motivations and intents
Harassment	A broad category that covers long-term hurtful or threatening messages/posts.	Anywhere online.	Personal grudges, mental illness, boredom, retaliation, failed relationship, and many more.
Doxing/outing	Revealing private information without consent. Sometimes this happens anonymously through a hacker or stranger.	Anonymously in a public forum or in an online private group. Sometimes the bully will directly send the private details to those who have a relationship with the victim. It can be common in gamer and hacker communities.	Annoyance with the user, failed relationship, a desire to show off in front of others, feeling like the victim "deserves" it.

Type of cyberbullying	What is it?	Where does it typically occur?	Potential motivations and intents
Trolling	Sharing and posting controversial and inflammatory comments online.	Popular in gamer communities and anonymous messaging boards like Reddit and 4chan.	For jokes and laughs, online credibility, boredom, a desire to share misinformation.
Trickery/ masquerading	Befriending and pretending to be someone they are not; this includes catfishing, which is a romantic deception.	Popular on Facebook and dating apps.	Financial gain (particularly in catfishing), boredom, a desire to hurt the victim, a joke.
Cyberstalking	This is a serious type that can include threats, monitoring accounts, false accusations, sexual harassment, and even offline stalking.	Various mediums. The perpetrator knows the victim, but the victim does not necessarily know the perpetrator.	Failed relationship, obsession with victim (particularly in celebrity cyberstalking), mental illness, feeling rejected, and/or wanting retaliation.

Dr. Justin Patchin of the Cyberbullying Research Institute said that between the different cyberbullying terms, "basically we're talking about hurtful behavior." He recommends that parents and educators ask children how they feel when being exposed to cyberbullying, and if children are engaging in behavior under that dark umbrella, ask them "How did you intend to make the other person feel by doing this?" "Whether you call it trolling or flaming, whatever the latest term," said Patchin, "it's about our behavior online and how that makes other people feel. It's perfectly fine to post a humorous inside joke or to be funny online, but you have to realize how that's going to make the other person feel."

This is a tricky subject, one that Patchin acknowledges adults struggle with. There's an argument made on the side of someone posting the joke, that others should try to assume best intent. That sometimes a joke is just a joke. The Internet is full of lapses in communication, where malicious intent can be ascribed through an email or post. Without inflections in voice or body language an email or post can seem passive aggressive or tone-deaf.

When someone is accused of or questioned about having bad intent online, they are less likely to listen to the other side. I remember this happening to me in an old job. I sent an email to some staff about a new project. I was trying to be very concise and direct in my email and wrote it out with bullet points and due dates. However, one member of staff interpreted that email as "bossy" and felt I was disrespectful. I was taken aside by my manager to discuss that communication. I remember feeling very frustrated in that conversation; I felt that unfair assumptions were made. I expressed a wish that the person had come to me directly, instead of bringing in a manager. Now, I was the one who felt disrespected.

Feelings matter, and so does intent. However, by ascribing "bossiness" or ill intent to my email, I felt less willing to work it out with the other person. If I had been approached and told, "I read your email and I think you meant well, but I felt it came across as bossy," I would have been more willing to listen and compromise. When someone says, "I feel" rather than "you are," that lowers the potential for defensiveness and fights. These types of miscommunication happen all the time online. Conflicts arise and are never resolved. When we give someone a label like "bossy, sexist, racist, rude," we may be speaking our feelings, but we don't give the other person an opportunity to listen or learn. Labels shut down the conversation and don't solve the conflict.

How do we balance assuming best intent, while still setting our own personal boundaries online and communicating how we feel? How do we express our feelings in a way that can be heard? The answer is . . . it depends. "If your kid comes to you and says that someone said something hurtful online, try to evaluate it objectively," said Patchin. Here are some questions to help you evaluate the situation:

- **Where did the incident happen? At school? In a game? In a private message?** If the negative message happened privately and directly, then there is little question about the intent. Intervention should happen swiftly. If cyberbullying happens at school, there are policies and practices to protect students. Gaming culture has different norms regarding cyberbullying which will be discussed later in Chapter 7 on page 133. Where/what platform cyberbullying occurs can give direction on the appropriate response.

- **Ask for clarification.** Instead of automatically assuming a negative intent, ask "What did you mean by that?" Don't ask a leading question like, "Why did you decide to be cruel and say that?" but ask something truly open-ended. Give the messenger an opportunity to explain the message. This tactic should be employed if there is a relationship between the child and the assumed cyberbully. If possible, ask the question in private. A public post to a comment can come across as confrontational.

- **Who is the person?** Is this someone who frequently posts controversial ideas or attacks others? If this is a pattern of behavior, depending on where it happens, either ignore it or report it; don't try to reason, or ask for clarification. If the comments that felt hurtful are out of the blue and this is irregular behavior, assume best intent. Check in with that person and ask, "Are you okay?"

- **How long has this been going on?** Is the cyberbullying a single post? Is there an extended period of messages and posts? Is your child being harassed on multiple platforms? If the harassment is persistent and long-term, more intervention is necessary and that harassment should be reported.

- **Self-reflect.** Examine your own feelings. Is there a reason
  this particular comment stung? Do you already have a
  negative relationship with this person? Sometimes when
  we have labeled someone a "troublemaker" or "dramatic,"
  anything they say, even if that wasn't the intent, can come
  across as hurtful.

When we are more reflective and less combative, we have emotional energy to respond to what life throws at us. If we are spending time reading into every comment, we're spending less time doing things that make us happy. We can easily become mired down and distracted with negativity on the Internet. Yes, there are definitely times to report and speak up, but also times to shrug it off and move on.

To be clear, the phrase "shrug it off" is not being dismissive of the very real effects of cyberbullying. There are connections between cyberbullying, poor academic performance, low self-esteem, and emotional and psychological problems. Cyberbullying can have long-term consequences on mental health. Cyberstalking, a type of cyberbullying, should be taken very seriously. But if we don't look beyond the screen, and instead blame cyberbullying for all of our teen's problems, we may miss other preexisting conditions and risk factors in their life: mental health, hormones, a fight with a friend, stress at home, sleep issues, and more.

Research reported by Kowalski and Limber in the *Journal of Adolescent Health* said, "Researchers have recognized that depression, anxiety, and low self-esteem may be both consequences of and precursors to bullying. Thus, children who are bullied may be more likely than others to develop problems with depression, anxiety, and low self-esteem. In other cases, these symptoms may signal to others that a child may be an "easy target." In other words, being bullied can affect mental health, which makes them easier targets for future bullying, which can affect their mental health further. In addition, having mental health issues makes the bullying worse, and can bring on future bullying. It's a vicious spiral. A parent who has a child with depression or anxiety will want to take online harassment very seriously. They should also monitor the harassment to be sure it doesn't escalate or continue.

As children emotionally mature, parents can play a vital role in asking the right questions to help them reframe their way of thinking and help them understand when to react and when to adapt. They can kindly guide them in looking beyond the words to the context and to the person. They can help their children identify and communicate their own feelings. This is tough work that can be difficult to master—but it's a goal that can bring peace to you and your child's life.

What Parents Can Do About Cyberbullying

I will never forget my first bullies. I was in kindergarten and feeling proud and grown-up that I was taking the bus to school by myself. As a five-year-old, I was unfamiliar with the rules of the school bus—one being that little kids, like myself, have to sit in the front. So, early in my bus-riding days, I plopped myself down in the back of the bus. The back of the bus was the domain of fifth graders, who did not like that this little girl was invading their territory. They let me know very quickly that I was not welcome, and I got off the bus that day and ran to my parents with tears in my eyes.

My parents gave me the advice they thought best, to ignore it. They said for me to tell those (very large) fifth graders the famous phrase, "sticks and stones can break my bones, but words can never hurt me." And I did just that. It did not end well. These preadolescents found it hilarious that a little kindergartener would tell them that. The back of the bus was filled with laughter. I blushed crimson and rode to school with my head down—and never sat in the back of the bus again that school year.

My parent's advice was not bad. It was well-meaning and logical to them. From their perspective, why would you worry about what others think? It was a waste of time and energy. Age had given them new perspectives and their worries involved bills and work, not other people's opinions. I am around the age my parents were when giving me that advice, and I can see their perspective. Why *should* you worry about what people think? Just live your life and move forward.

But my adult brain still remembers being bullied. We, as adults, have the benefits of hindsight and experience, but we are hampered to help our children by our emotional states. While I can still remember the bullies, the feelings when retrieving that memory are different from experiencing it. We can understand our child's present through our past, but it's not through the same lens. This means that our advice around incidents like bullying, although given with love and caring, may not be helpful in the moment.

Dr. Patchin reminds parents of this developmental disconnect:

> A lot of times when kids are cyberbullied their parents are going to take away the technology or tell them to suck it up. I think we're getting better as parents at recognizing the harm involved in cyberbullying. When I talk to parents, I tell them that it's hard for us to understand that harm because we're thinking about it from our adult brain. When you're an adolescent it's all about what others think about them. When a kid is being mean to another kid our adult brain thinks, "just ignore it," but that's not possible for a kid brain. No matter what your child says to you about bullying or cyberbullying, even if it doesn't sound that big of a deal to you, if it's gotten to the point where they've come to you, it's a big deal.

What can parents do to help their children deal with cyberbullying? "Give them tools to deal with it," says Patchin. Here are some potential tools for parents:

- Provide a space for children to vent and express their feelings. Listen to your child without interruptions or explaining away their feelings.

- Encourage your child to take action. Coax them to talk to a teacher or a principal. Have them take screenshots of the cyberbullying.
- Don't wait. Take action immediately. The cyberbullying does not necessarily go away on its own.
- Suggest having your child write in a journal about their feelings and the incidents. In the worst-case scenario, this journal can help law enforcement if the bullying escalates.
- Teach your child coping strategies like meditative practices, reframing the scenario in their head, self-reflecting, and more.

Parents of tweens and teenagers should take the role of a mentor and try to refrain from rushing into battle and taking over. "It's more important at that age to give them some agency," said Patchin. He also recommends keeping the lines of communication open, which means parents must talk less and listen more. "In the elementary school years, they are most bonded to the parents whereas in middle adolescence they are moving away from parents to their peer group," says Patchin. Peers can be a great support to older children when cyberbullying occurs. They can give advice, defend, speak up for their friends, and more. Parents should encourage those relationships and suggest that even if their teen doesn't want to talk to them about the problem, they hope they can talk to their friends.

Sometimes friend groups are the problem. This puts parents in a difficult position because friends can be both a risk factor and a protective factor. And sometimes the same friend both encourages risky behavior and provides emotional support. This means that cutting off a friend who is not the best influence can leave your teen lonelier.

Patchin also gives recommendations for how to talk about bullying with adolescents. "With a high schooler I don't know if I would use the word bullying. For better or worse, it has a negative connotation to it, a 'kid problem' even though we use the term for workplace bullying as well." I have seen this in my own work with teens. They may roll their eyes at the word. Since elementary school they have attended anti-bullying assemblies or gotten lectures from adults. My staff and I try to use the term "bullying" sparingly, instead referring to "school or relationship problems" when working with middle- and high-school students. "A kid might come and say 'drama' on Instagram. They definitely won't use the term bullying unless it's a really bad situation. They will use the word 'hurt' or 'hurtfulness,'" says Patchin.

Whether it is hurt, problems, drama, or bullying, parents can be placed in a difficult situation when trying to help their children. They may have intense emotional protective reactions or they may be confused as to what the fuss is all about. Parents are working from their own perspectives with their adult brain. That adult brain is great at long-term forecasting and can better see the big picture, but it isn't so great at empathizing with their child's experience; while they can see that their child is hurting, they can't *feel* that hurt. This means that parents need to step back from their initial response and address the issue with listening and skill-building. Here are some questions to help parents pause, listen, and choose next steps when cyberbullying occurs:

- What does my child need right this second?
- How can I encourage my child to process their feelings?
- What evidence may I need from this incident if it escalates?
- What are some moderation tools on this platform that my child can use?
- How would a ____ year-old feel about this cyberbullying?
- Does my child need to speak to a teacher/principal?

Online Privacy

I've taught hundreds of K-12 students in the last few years and over that time I've realized that they think of privacy differently than I do. They are good at knowing the basics like don't share your personal information with strangers, but they don't think about privacy in terms of tracking, data collection, and the information they are giving to private companies. I think part of the reason for this is that they have grown up with a different Internet than you and me.

I'm a Millennial and joined the early Internet in my elementary years. I confess that I have actually used the phrase "surfing the web." It was more fragmented and freer back then. The think tank Freedom House creates an annual report on Internet freedoms and, sadly, for the third year in a row, reported that Internet in the United States is less and less free. This definition of freedom includes access, expression, and privacy. It also includes monitoring, and the 2019 report "found that 89 percent of all Internet users are subject to advanced social media monitoring systems implemented by their own governments, the equivalent of roughly 3 billion people." Governments are not the only one's monitoring, it's big business.

The Internet when I was young, and perhaps when you were, too, was one of colorful and often flashing web pages made by users with pages and pages of links. I spent time in newsgroups and chat rooms, but you had to work harder to find them since Google was not ubiquitous. The massive companies of today like Amazon and Google were young and there was a wide space for new start-ups and ideas. The World Wide Web was also smaller, some estimates say there were just 10,000 websites in 1994, and dial-up was the only way to get online. Here are some stats that describe the 2020s Internet as compared to the 1990s.

- Over one third of all websites use WordPress to manage their content.
- About two thirds of people browsing the Internet use Google Chrome as their main browser.
- About 94 percent of users globally use Google to make mobile web searches.
- Facebook is the fourth most visited website in the world.
- YouTube was the number one downloaded app across the globe in 2019.

While the web was smaller in the 1990s, it had more diversity, and less monitoring. Children and teens have no experience with the first version of the Internet. Their Internet is faster, mobile, and dominated by huge tech companies. They have little to no expectations of privacy because they don't know anything different. How do parents communicate about privacy in a world where there is less privacy online than ever before?

According to some researchers and policy makers, there is not just one Internet. The splInternet, also called "Internet balkanization" is the term given to dividing and splintering of the Internet because of divergent political, commercial, and national interests.

In a commercial sense, the splInternet refers to technological ecosystems that keep users in one controlled platform. Think about your own tech use. If you have a Chromebook, you probably use Google Chrome, Android mobile operating systems, download from the Google Play store, and more. The devices, operating systems, and platforms we utilize can limit our use of the Internet. Using just one commercial product can also limit us privacy-wise. We have fewer choices and options if we are forced or choose to use just one company's system.

More recently, the term splInternet refers to political and national divisions in technology, most notably in China. The term the "Great Firewall" refers to China's technological ecosystem which blocks other types of tech from entering its borders. In China, there are many blocked sites, apps, and software including Google, YouTube, Facebook, Netflix, Wikipedia, Instagram, Twitter, Twitch, and news sites. China's firewall also affects its citizens' privacy who are forced to use certain apps which collect their data.

Every country has their own online restrictions and laws. Some, like China, are more restrictive than others. Unfortunately for online privacy, the worldwide trend has been less, not more, privacy. When discussing online privacy, parents should consider talking about how privacy is a freedom and a right, and it can be taken away.

Thinking about Online Privacy More Broadly

Tech trends have changed the landscape of online privacy—but parental education lags behind. While the basics of online privacy should be taught, it's insufficient. When online privacy is taught, it's often around the individual. We tell children "Don't share your info with strangers," "Don't share your password," "Don't put your credit card information online." That's good advice, but it's focused on an individual rather than a systems approach. It puts the onus and responsibility on the person, often a child, rather than governments and technology companies to adjust their privacy rules.

Companies have taken children's data without permission, had breaches of this data, and frequently try to work around government regulations. Children's data is surveilled through educational apps, games, and software they are forced to use. Children's rights have been subverted for market share. And despite these violations, the focus has still been on educating individuals rather than reforming the system.

Sonia Livingstone is a researcher and professor of social psychology at the London School of Economics (LSE). She studies and writes about online privacy and safety. Livingstone suggests expanding our conceptualization of online privacy. She writes on the LSE blog, "Privacy depends on the context. For our child-rights approach, it valuably sidesteps the popular charge that children (foolishly) either seek or eschew *secrecy*, this in turn seeming to support the popular call on parents to *control* them." Online privacy changes in different contexts, but we typically only speak about it when it comes to children's relationships with others (i.e., "Don't talk to strangers!") From her research, Livingstone finds that young people "often care deeply about what personal information is shared with their friends or parents" but "they cannot imagine why the huge corporations which own Instagram or Snapchat, for example, would be interested in them. Nor, for different reasons, do they expect to worry that trusted institutions (school, doctor) would share their personal information with others." Her and other's studies find that children have a basic understanding of the dangers of sharing data in these interpersonal contexts, but struggle to understand them in institutional and commercial contexts. For example, a tween may know not to share their name on Fortnite, but they don't think twice about the data they're sharing with their playing and purchasing on the site.

How can parents help children protect their privacy beyond the interpersonal? This is difficult because to function in society there is a certain amount of data that you will be forced to provide. Workplaces require certain software. Schools test online. Purchases, bill paying, research, and so much happen online and a certain amount of data sharing is unavoidable. Unless you move into the forest completely unplugged, you are forced to interact with the data ecosystem.

But there are some steps that parents and caregivers can take:

- **Talk about online advertising with children.** Help children understand that celebrities and influencers are often being paid to tweet or post about products. These may not be labeled advertisements, but they serve the same purpose.
- **Change browsing habits.** Instead of Google Chrome, the world's most popular browser, use a service like DuckDuckGo or Privacy Badger that does not track search terms. If you are searching on a larger browser like Chrome, use Incognito mode, or a plug-in that blocks pop-ups and cookies.
- **Understand the laws.** The United States has a patchwork of privacy laws around children. The Federal Trade Commission

is the agency primarily dedicated to what data websites can collect from children. The Children's Online Privacy Protection Act (COPPA) gives parents and caregivers some control over what data can be collected. The European Union has a more robust privacy act, General Data Protection Regulation (GDPR), that also has guidance for parents.

- **Look into other children's privacy resources.** Some additional resources for parents on this topic are the Electronic Frontier Foundation, the National Cyber Security Alliance, Consumer Report's Digital Lab, which investigates privacy practices, and the Federal Trade Commission, which has advice for parents and a place to report online privacy violations.

There has been pushback on online privacy in recent years. YouTube paid $170 million for alleged violations of children's privacy in 2019 and shifted how they categorized videos aimed at minors. There is a current class-action lawsuit against TikTok for taking children's data and sending it to China. Both Google and Facebook are in a lawsuit with the US government over their business practices. Facebook settled a lawsuit in 2020 about biometric data it obtained without consent.

Improvements in machine learning and the growth of data online has made it easier for that data to be categorized, stored, and patterned. A concerning tech trend impacting online privacy is the growth and advance of biometrics. Biometrics refers to the measurement of specific characteristics of people such as fingerprints, facial recognition, iris recognition, DNA, voice, typing rhythm, and more. If you have a fingerprint password on your phone, you've had biometrics

(Continued on next page)

used on you. If you say, "Okay, Google" and ask your smart device to play something, that involves biometrics of voice. Biometrics are used online to prevent fraud and speed up identification, but can also be used in political and dehumanizing ways. For example, in China, technology start-ups built algorithms used to track ethnic Muslims, who have been corralled into detention camps and abused.

Biometrics present several privacy concerns. This data may be obtained without consent or through unintended scope. For example, if law enforcement is looking for a suspect in a crowd, others in the crowd may have been surveilled without their knowledge. Biometrics could also be taken from minors without parental consent. Critics in the United States have said that biometrics may violate the fourth amendment of the Constitution, prohibiting searches and seizures. There are local and federal lawsuits against and investigations into biometrics around the world, particularly the use of facial recognition.

Modeling Online Privacy at Home

To be fair, young people are not alone in their lack of understanding regarding cybersecurity and online privacy. A Pew Research study in 2019 reported that "while a majority of US adults can correctly answer questions about phishing scams or website cookies, other items are more challenging." The report gives the example of two-factor authentication, where you must log in to an account in more than one way, as a mystery to almost three-quarters of Americans. Additionally, only "about one-quarter of Americans (24 percent) know that private browsing only hides browser history from other users of that computer." So, you may think you're being private, and you may be on that particular device, but outside companies still monitor you. Out of the ten questions about cybersecurity and the business side of social media companies, only 2 percent of Americans got all ten questions right.

Adults are also not modeling online privacy to their children. We have expectations that children do not talk to strangers, do not post revealing information, and stay out of certain corners of the Internet. Those are realistic expectations and important rules. But if we are not showing that we care about privacy and can follow our own rules—why would they listen? If you tell your daughter not to post revealing photos on Instagram, but you post your own, why would she listen? If you tell your son he tweets too much, but on your account, you tweet throughout the day, why would he do what you say? We need to reflect on our own behaviors. We also need to consider consent. At a certain age, we need to ask our children permission. They have their own lives, friends, interests, and preferences that should be taken into consideration. Ask yourself these questions:

- Am I asking permission to post about my child?
- Am I sharing too much information about myself online?
- Do I regularly share family photos with my child in them? Does my child know I share these photos?
- Why do I share information/photos of my child? What is my motivation?
- If my child told me I could not share information about them, how would that make me feel?
- How would it make me feel if my child shared pictures of me without my consent?

Dr. Livingstone writes in a 2018 literature review of children's data that online privacy is "no longer about discipline and control alone," and cautions that "risk aversion, however, restricts children's play, development, and agency, and constrains their exploration of physical, social, and virtual worlds." Like with all issues of online safety, parents must walk the difficult line between protection and prevention and exploration. Livingstone goes on to write:

While the task of balancing children's independence and protection is challenging, evidence suggests that good support can make an important difference to children's privacy online. Restrictive parenting has a suppressive effect, reducing privacy and other risks but also impeding the benefits of Internet use. Enabling mediation, on the other hand, is more empowering in allowing children to engage with social networks.

In some ways, it's easier to be restrictive. It requires less talking and thinking. Just ban it or block it and the thinking is done. But this is a false security. Parents should be having discussions, researching digital products, understanding laws, modeling good behavior, and adjusting our settings.

Sexting

Sexting is a topic that comes up frequently in my work with parents, principals, and law enforcement. There are legal and other consequences of sexting between minors, which I'll address later in this chapter, but I'm going to bring up another side of sexting first. One that may be controversial. When I was researching for my previous book called *Becoming a Digital Parent: A Practical Guide to Help Families Navigate Technology*, I came across work out of the Cyberbullying Research Center on "safe sexting." They describe it as "generally speaking, emphasizing avoidance of risky sexual behaviors via abstention has proven ineffectual. It is time to move beyond abstinence-only, fear-based sexting education (or worse yet, no education at all)."

For this book I had the opportunity to interview Dr. Patchin, the codirector and coauthor of that earlier-mentioned article on safe sexting. I was eager to ask about the reactions to his work. He said, "I had so many parents email me based on the title of the article and just go off, 'there's no such thing as safe sexting,' 'how would you feel if your kid did that?' But I had to reply, 'read the article, of course I wouldn't want my child to sext, but if he chose to do so and followed the recommendations in our paper, I wouldn't mind it.'" I agree with Dr. Patchin, I wouldn't want my son to sext either. But I understand that one day he'll reach sexual maturity, get into serious relationships, and have a desire to share thoughts and desires. Those desires are normal and part of growing up. I want him to feel comfortable expressing his feelings in a consensual and respectful way, and not feel shame having sexual thoughts.

The discussions and education around sexting can involve blaming or shaming. ("You made a mistake and here is the punishment," "You should have just said no.") This abstinence-only approach can affect a young person's mental health. A study published in *PLOS One* examined how adolescents use a wide range of emotional regulation strategies, and how that affects how they deal with shame. The researchers describe shame as involving "negative evaluations of the global self and is accompanied by a sense of inferiority and worthlessness, and the desire to escape and hide." They point out that shame and guilt can serve social goals. Perhaps I make an offhand comment online and someone speaks up that it hurt them. If I feel guilt from that encounter, I may resolve to do better next time and apologize. But the researchers point out that a "disproportionate" amount of shame or guilt can cause "negative outcomes such as anxiety and depression, eating disorders, delinquent behavior, and substance abuse."

In short, a little guilt can help redirect a person—but a lot of guilt can redirect that person in a downward spiral. This downward spiral is fueled by catastrophizing, basically assuming the worst will happen. A person who feels a disproportionate amount of guilt from sexting, whether from peers, parents, or a well-meaning educational program may say to themselves, *I screwed up. Everyone knows. I can't go to school now.* This unhealthy coping mechanism can bring on depression and anxiety. Thus, educators and parents need to be careful in the way we talk about sexting. If we treat sexting as a big thing that will affect the rest of your life, some adolescents, still learning proper emotional regulation skills, will internalize those messages.

The messages of safe sexting are focused on the big picture. Dr. Patchin uses the analogy of a storm: "If it's stormy outside you don't tell your kid don't go outside, you'll get struck by lightning. It does happen every day, but it's more likely they're going to get wet, get sick, wreck their clothes." Parents shouldn't catastrophize snakes, storms, or sexting.

Patchin describes the process of getting the word out about his safe sexting article:

> We sent it first to a journal of Australia to review. It almost got published in the first place we sent it, in a huge journal, but the editorial people said they didn't want to do it. Then one journal gave us feedback, and it definitely got us thinking more about the prosocial aspect of sexting. The point is, if you have two consenting, not in an illegal standpoint, sixteen-year-olds, seventeen-year-olds who share these images with each other and they don't go beyond that relationship—here's trust, there's consent, it's within the consent of the relationship—BIG DEAL. What is the big deal? It's a citation, like an underage drinking ticket, we really don't want our kids doing it, but maybe it's a part of a healthy adult relationship, maybe it's a healthy thing like drinking in the right context as an appropriate and socially acceptable thing. We started to reevaluate our opinions on our behaviors once we learned more about them and studied some of the research. Society is not ready for this type of conversation, but our paper is an effort to push that in a different direction. I think in twenty years we'll look at our paper and think it's quaint.

Perhaps Patchin is right, society may not be ready for this conversation, but these conversations are being had. And parents and educators should reevaluate the messages we are sending to our youth.

Sexting, like other sexual practices, has a double standard for men and women. Society expects men and women to follow a sexual script. When partners follow this script, it can decrease uncertainty and anxiety. These scripts are created through societal, religious, and cultural expectations. In addition, the media teaches us what to expect. Think of a TV show or movie you've watched. Typically, the man will pursue the woman, pay for dinner on a date, and initiate sexual contact.

Two research studies to date demonstrate what happens when women do not follow this sexual script when sexting. When men solicited sexts, they were viewed as masculine and gained peer approval by tagging and sending pictures. If a woman sends a sext she is thought of as shameful, and less intelligent. This sexual double standard (SDS) means that men and boys can gain status through sexting, but women and girls cannot do the same.

However, this sexual double standard is fading according to research published in the summer of 2020 in the journal *Sexuality & Culture*. A study of about 1,000 US adults in their thirties had more neutral feelings toward those who sexted. "The results suggest that sexting is viewed as a more normative sexual behavior instead of a risky sexual practice," the researchers write. "Additionally, the results suggest that the traditional SDS may no longer appear in relation to sexting . . . reflecting societal changes toward this behavior."

Parents have to determine their own norms and values in their families, and these may push against existing societal changes and norms. These norms are changing as younger generations become more familiar with technology. If adults in their thirties currently have fewer negative views on sexting than before, how will teens view sexting in 10–20 years?

Safe sexting is a harm reduction approach. It does not encourage sexting but acknowledges that it may happen and seeks to reduce potential negative consequences. Here are some themes paraphrased from Patchin's safe sexting article published in the *Journal of Adolescent Health*. These are guidelines that parents and caregivers can share with youth.

- Do not send nude images to someone who you are not 100 percent certain would like to see it.
- Trust those who you send sexts to.
- Do not share sexts you receive with anyone else.
- Turn off your device's location services for all your social media apps and make sure that any photos are not tagged with your location, username, or the date.
- Consider sending suggestive or flirty pictures instead of nudes.
- Never include your face in a sext, and be careful not to send pictures that can identify you through birthmarks, tattoos, or your surroundings in the picture.
- If you are being pressured or threatened to send nude photos, collect digital evidence.
- Delete explicit photos and videos from your device.

Dr. Patchin encourages others to "read the piece and think thoughtfully for and what we're trying to prevent. We're trying to prevent the worst consequences." Those consequences can be legal troubles. US sexting laws vary in each state, depending on what type of nudes were shared and with whom. Laws around minors sexting can differ in other countries as well. Under the 1978 Protection of Children Act in England and Wales, over 6,000 children have been investigated by the police from 2016–2019. These laws are currently being debated in different states and countries.

Another "worst consequence" is sextortion. A study of sextortion of minors in the *Journal of Adolescent Health* found that fear of the consequences of sexting may make young people feel "trapped" after sending an explicit image. This can make them more vulnerable to online predators. Young people who are scared, anxious, and feeling shamed want to hide. In that situation, they may be more likely to "cooperate" and send more nudes or participate in other acts so that their sexting pictures are hidden from family and friends.

Patchin echoes some of my feelings around sexting, saying, "I'm not looking forward to having these conversations with my kid." But he acknowledges, "It's reality. It's just the nature of the beast, when technology evolves and society evolves you have to evolve with it. That's not to sacrifice your values and your morals, but to look at the full picture, we have to realize what's going on and minimize harm."

Pornography

In my work with Digital Respons-Ability, I found myself inadvertently thrust into the anti-porn space. I was once asked to be on a panel with staff from an anti-pornography nonprofit and have participated in community discussions and meetings with anti-porn advocates. While I do not bring up pornography in my parenting presentations, the question does come up. Through conversations and research, I have discovered many people who associate online safety with anti-pornography.

I do not bring up pornography in my parenting presentations because it is a highly politicized and controversial topic. Your opinions about pornography depend on your upbringing, race, religion, political affiliation, sexuality, and much more. It's also a subject that needs more research and longitudinal studies. In a 2018 study in the *Journal of Sex Research*, researchers looked at the pornography use of 900 people from adolescence through adulthood. They found associations between pornography use and mental health but did not find that pornography use in adolescence directly translated to the same pattern of consumption in adulthood. In their review of pornography literature, these researchers write, "the research on pornography and its correlates is mixed and varied." The researchers encourage looking at pornography within the context of both the individual and their life circumstances:

> These mixed findings have suggested to many scholars that pornography use likely does not have a universally positive or negative effect on the individuals that view it. Several contextual factors likely come into play that shift and alter the effect based on the individual, relational, and cultural differences. For example, a consumer of pornography embedded in a religious culture that perceives such use as a violation of moral standards may misinterpret that individual's normative use as compulsive and addictive, despite relatively low frequency.

You may view pornography differently in a relationship other than single. It affects adolescents differently than adults, and men differently than women. As a parent, it's important to keep in mind that pornography may or may not affect your child the same as other children. You should know your child and their risk factors and that should inform your conversations with them.

The biggest reason pornography is not part of my digital parenting trainings is that I do not feel it needs to be separately addressed. If you are already teaching your children skills from the 3 Ms like self-regulation, setting boundaries, and watching your digital footprint, you're helping them navigate pornography online. In addition to providing regular and robust sexual education, parents should talk about pornography the same way they do other online dangers. Sexual education is addressed more in Chapter 5 on page 65.

Pornography is a big part of the Internet and young people will come across it, so it is something to discuss and be concerned about. Parents should not be ignoring the millions of hours of pornography content online. That would be like ignoring the dancing and singing elephant in the corner of the room. But they should look at porn in the context of their own children. Children are unique and some have risk factors that can lead to pornography having a more negative impact on their lives. Other children may not have much interest in it at all so it will never become an issue.

What are these risk and protective factors of pornography? A systematic review of the literature from 2005–2016 summarized some of these.

Risk and Protective Factors of Pornography Consumption

Risk Factors	Protective Factors
Family conflict, family history of pornography use	Family connectedness
Availability of pornographic materials	Programs that support healthy norms such as Internet safety presentations
Experienced child abuse	Positive family life
Peers/friends who engage in pornography	Positive peer role models
Low caregiver monitoring or frequent coercive discipline	Positive parenting style
Male	Female
Little or no attachment to school	Positive and close attachments to school

The highest risk group for pornography use are boys aged 13–15 or children who have experienced abuse or neglect at home. The biggest protective factor to prevent or lessen pornography use are positive and close attachments to family, friends, and community. Thus, the best way you can protect children from porn is to love and support them.

Pornography and Gender

Boys are the main users of pornography and, unfortunately, many learn about sex this way. Pornography is very gendered and supports traditional gender norms of control and sexual conquest. Like sexting, pornography has sexual scripts that reflect societal and cultural norms of behavior. Dr. Tara Emmers-Sommer, a researcher in sex and gender issues, describes these pornography scripts:

Much of the mainstream pornography follows much of the same pattern, a pattern in which the man's sexual appetite is the one that is fed; the man's sexual desires are what prevail and, the desires are often met by one or more women in the material. That said, sexually explicit media by women for women, where the woman's sexual desires and script are front and center, do exist. However, this type of script is less predominant in the prevailing cultural script in pornography, despite women consuming pornography for personal reasons.

Teen boys who consume a great deal of pornography may internalize more beliefs in traditional and unhealthy gender norms. A literature review of pornography from 1995–2015 published in the *Journal of Sex Research* found that pornography consumption is associated with adherence to gender-stereotypical beliefs, resulting in a higher likelihood of boys engaging in sexual aggression. Emmers-Sommer backs up these findings through her research with college-aged men and women:

> Men who are current consumers of porn also reported higher adversarial sexual attitudes and rape myth acceptance (RMA) than women who are current consumers of porn. Past research demonstrates connections between consumption of sexual material, particularly sexually violent media and RMA and these findings hold for men and women, although more pronounced for men.

I should make a note that pornography research in general is full of correlations. Just because there are "connections" between pornography consumption does not mean that if you consume pornography you hold more negative gender stereotypes and beliefs.

A summary of the harmful hetero-normative themes of porn include:

- All women want sex from all men.

- Men are the sexual subject and women the sexual object.
- Men's pleasure comes first.
- Women want all types of sex acts from men, even if they are aggressive or humiliating.
- If a woman resists sex, she can be persuaded to change her mind.

Many of the conversations I've had about pornography touch on morality, but I think gender is an important missing piece of these conversations. While parents and pastors can debate the morality of pornography, there is less debate around the often-sexist themes in porn. These themes affect boys and girls. A boy may feel like his penis needs to be larger or that he is less of a man if a woman takes the lead in sexual activity. A girl may get the message that her own sexual pleasure and feelings about sex are not important. For both girls and boys, pornography can create unrealistic expectations about sex, how to look, how to act, and push unhealthy sexual scripts on vulnerable young people.

Internet porn is a monopoly dominated by the Canadian-owned MindGeek. MindGeek owns the sites: Pornhub, RedTube, Xtube, Brazzers, over 100 websites. Pornhub attracts 3.5 billion visits a month, more than Amazon or Netflix. According to an article in Mashable by Jess Joho, "MindGeek has a vast amount of power and influence over porn industry actors and producers." Monopolies are good for companies, not the people who work for them. MindGeek and its largest "tube" site Pornhub profits off piracy of other sites' videos and those videos are not always legal.

While MindGeek tries to take down illegal content, it's not always clear what age the performers are or if they were

(Continued on next page)

sex trafficked. Another issue with Pornhub is that, unlike YouTube, videos there can be downloaded. This means even if a video is flagged and taken off the site, it can still pop up elsewhere, or even on the Dark Web. While the vast majority of content uploaded to Pornhub is legal, there is still child pornography uploaded that escapes the notice of MindGeek's (too few) moderators. Consumers may inadvertently be watching pornography that involves coercion, children, or illegal practices. It also affects the performers. When online porn is free and easily accessible, it makes it harder for performers' rights, safety, and consent to be protected.

Porn Literacy

As with other digital behaviors, we should look at the why. A 2018 study of twelfth graders through age twenty-five found that the biggest reason male participants said they watched pornography was "curiosity" followed by "friends were watching." Curiosity is normal, just like a teen wanting to fit in with their friends. This natural instinct to understand and learn is in all children but, unfortunately, these children's friends and porn sites are not the best teachers.

Some school districts and countries are offering pornography education. A porn literacy program in Boston provided a nine-part media literacy curriculum on pornography between 2016 and 2019. This program for high schoolers "was designed to change beliefs about, for example, performing in pornography being an easy way to become wealthy, or pornography being realistic." The curriculum had a nonjudgmental approach to sexual behaviors and interests. The intent was not designed to be "abstinence-only" and stop porn use. It was to educate, raise discussions, and change beliefs and stereotypes. Researchers found that the adolescents who participated in this program experienced "changes in knowledge, attitudes, and behavioral intensions related to pornography" and they found that it did not increase any consumption of pornography by the students.

Porn literacy is a controversial and new topic. More research is needed. Some countries and organizations are more involved in porn literacy like New Zealand, Denmark, the state of Oregon, and Sweden, but overall, this is an area with no set curriculum standards, few practitioners, and even fewer opportunities to teach. If parents are wanting to educate their children more on pornography, here are some resources to consider:

- *For Goodness Sex: Changing the Way We Talk to Teens about Sexuality, Values, and Health* by Al Vernacchio
- The Porn Conversation: http://thepornconversation.org
- *Sex, Teens, and Everything in Between: The New and Necessary Conversations Today's Teenagers Need to Have about Consent, Sexual Harassment, Healthy Relationships, Love, and More* by Shafia Zaloom
- *Sexual Decisions: The Ultimate Teen Guide* by L. Kris Gowen
- Rights, Respect, Responsibility is a sex education curriculum that meets the National Sexuality Education Standards and is free to download: https://3rs.org/3rs-curriculum/

Young people should think critically about what online content they consume, and the effects it can have on others and themselves. Pornography can cause harm, but sometimes those harms are exaggerated. A real harm is the shame that adolescents may feel when they watch porn. A study published in 2017 in the *Journal of Sex Research* found that those who define themselves as religious were more likely to overestimate the harm and shame of watching pornography, experience greater distress related to their porn consumption, and more likely to call themselves "addicts." It's not necessarily the pornography use that causes problems, the study says, but the shame around that use that can heighten anxiety and increase depression. If someone believes that porn is inherently bad, that it's a black-and-white issue with no nuance, they are more likely to experience shame. But if a child has exposure to looking at pornography critically, is supported rather than shamed by parents, and does not believe that pornography always causes problems, they will be less likely to feel distressed and will suffer less harm.

Most sex trafficking, the illegal business of grooming, acquiring, then transporting people for sex, happens online. According to the nonprofit We are Thorn, 75 percent of sex trafficking survivors reported that they were advertised online. There are some beliefs, encouraged by conspiracy theories like QAnon, that children are simply taken off the streets and trafficked. While this does happen, it's rare, and children are most likely to be trafficked by someone they know like a family member or boyfriend.

Some children are at much greater risk to be sex trafficked than others. Risk factors include:

- Victim of child abuse.
- Runaway or homeless youth.
- LGBTQ youth are about five times more likely than heterosexuals to be victims of trafficking.
- Youth in foster care.
- Adolescent female.
- Child who has lived or currently lives with someone with substance abuse issues.

The National Center for Missing & Exploited Children recommends that parents "monitor what your child does and who your child is interacting with on the Internet." They also describe the importance of communication. "Open communication is key. Help make your children more aware by explaining the dangers of sex trafficking and by challenging myths and misconceptions that glamorize commercial sex." As mentioned earlier, sex workers are mostly poorly paid and work in unsafe conditions. Also communicate to your children your jurisdiction's laws around sexting. Although it has become less common, a minor can be accused of child sex trafficking. In some places, if you are under eighteen years old and take a picture of yourself nude and share it, your careless mistake can become a child sex trafficking offense.

Red Flag Apps

I often end my digital parenting presentations by discussing red flag apps. I use the words "red flag" because just because someone uses a particular app or behaves in a certain way does not mean that they are necessarily engaging in unhealthy behaviors. Correlation does not mean causation. But red flags are important to monitor. I am regularly changing my list of red flag apps in presentations. Some of these apps are like weeds. They get pulled up but sprout up again in another form. Apps come and go, and it can be hard for parents to keep on top of trends. I tell parents that it's less important to know the names of the apps than it is to know the categories and that they're out there. For this section I will share some specific names of apps but will focus more on the categories of apps since they quickly evolve and change.

Random and Anonymous Chat Apps

At a presentation last year with school counselors, I talked about random and anonymous chat apps. These apps will pair random strangers over text or video to communicate. With these apps, you can narrow down who you want to talk to but you won't know for certain who will be on the other end. After describing these apps, I asked the group if there were any questions. A woman raised her hand. She had a perplexed look on her face and asked, "But why would someone use an app like this?" "Good question," I told her.

As adults, it's hard to wrap our heads around this desire for strangeness, variety, and chance. But adolescents think differently.

As described in Chapter 5 on page 65, teen brains are wired for risk. They experience a higher dopamine reward when they do something dangerous. Talking to a random stranger online is exciting to them, while for an adult it may be confusing and uncomfortable.

There are serious concerns with these random chat apps. One is a lack of moderation. The most infamous of random chat apps was Chatroulette. Started in 2009 by a teenager, Chatroulette was the first random video chat app. It quickly became popular, and quickly had issues. There was absolutely no moderation in the beginning, and obscene and pornographic materials could easily be found on the site. Minors could be paired with adults that groomed or preyed on children.

Since Chatroulette there have been numerous other random chat apps. Some of these are text-only and some have more controls over who the user is paired with. There are random chat apps for dating and hookups as well.

Some other random chat apps that are currently out there include:

- HOLLA
- Chitter
- Chatous
- Omegle
- Wakie

Parents should be aware that the same functions of these random chats can be found on mainstream apps. When Chatroulette was created by then-teen Andrey Ternovsky, nothing else similar existed. Ternovsky said that "this idea popped into his head from Skype's video conferencing function." Since 2009, there are many more video conferencing options than just Skype. Plus, platforms like Facebook, Snapchat, and Discord all offer similar tools. That's one reason I put the usage of these apps as a red flag. If I just wanted to video chat with a friend, there are many other ways to do it. By downloading one of these apps, I have certain intentions.

Anonymous Online Forums

An anonymous online forum, also called a discussion board, discussion group, or newsgroup is a text-based platform that keeps postings online for a period of time. This is in contrast to a chat room, which occurs in real-time and you have to be present to read them. There are many text-based online forums and the large majority are harmless. Many are based on a particular topic, like a game, where gamers ask questions and post comments. Others are for troubleshooting, like the site GitHub that, along with other services, has over 100 million repositories and is the largest host of source code in the world. You may have used one of these forums/repositories when you had issues with a printer or a home appliance and wanted help on how to fix it. These online forums are not always anonymous, but for the most part can be browsed anonymously. I do not have to create an account to read posts or other information.

The red flag anonymous online forums I mention to parents and educators are:

- **4chan**: This anonymous online forum is linked to hate speech, conspiracy theories, revenge porn, and many other dangerous and illegal online behaviors.
- **8kun**: Formerly 8chan, this spin-off of 4chan currently exists on the Dark Web since being kicked off its Cloudflare hosting platform. According to one anonymous long-time 4chan user, "4channers hate 8chan. It's the worst of the worst."
- **Kiwi Farms**: This site is a stalking forum focused on attacking "lolcows." The term lolcow is a spin on "cash cow" that refers to targets, typically celebrities, that users can keep making fun of for the laughs.

Two other forums I don't include on my red flag list deserve a mention: Something Awful and Reddit. Both I do not include on the list because the bulk of their platform is informational and often helpful.

As an active Reddit user, I have found helpful advice on business, finance, law, and health—along with posts that make me troubled. Something Awful, the precursor of 4chan, is not on my list since it has evolved since its early days and, like Reddit, has informational boards. Unlike Reddit, Something Awful is far less moderated and should be viewed with caution.

Online forums have existed since the early days of the Internet. It was where I spent most of my time in the 1990s. I would chat on different fandom groups and often wade into random chat rooms for fun. I have to cringe a little thinking that here I am telling parents to monitor and watch communications on online forums when I was heavily using them during my preadolescent years, despite my parents' concern. (Sorry, Mom, you were right!) There is much more to say about these red flag forums through a lens of media literacy, fake news, and communication. I do a deeper dive into these in Chapter 8 on page 167.

End-to-End Encryption Communication Apps

End-to-end encryption (E2EE) is a system of communication that limits potential eavesdropping between others (besides the individuals communicating). In messaging systems like email and other chat networks, messages may pass through or be stored by third parties. Then, the recipient retrieves the message from those groups. End-to-end encryption also uses protocols that can prevent messages from being modified or read. Using E2EE can prevent against cyberattacks and is a secure way of communicating online. It's a communication system I use regularly myself and have recommended to others. However, the use of E2EE, particularly by minors, can be a red flag.

If you are hiding something, you're more likely to use E2EE. This type of communication has been utilized for illegal means, like with hackers and hate groups. For example, neo-Nazis and fascist hate groups used Telegram to organize a gun rally in January 2020. As of this writing, the Boogaloo Bois, a violent right-wing extremist group, runs large channels on this same app. End-to-end encryption apps are also frequently used for hookups, like on the popular app Kik, to protect identities of users and to hide information. I use these apps because I'm concerned about online privacy, but your average fourteen-year-old may not feel that way.

If your child is using any one of these apps regularly, you should be on alert and monitor the situation:

- Telegram
- Signal
- Wickr
- Wire

Apps can be used to organize violent protests or organize help for a neighbor. Like many subjects discussed in this chapter, software, platforms, apps, and other digital technologies have the capacity for caring or hurting. They're like snakes. For the most part, you don't see snakes, they leave people alone. Only a few varieties will bite you, and only a few of those will poison you. We should take precautions with snakes such as wearing the proper shoes and knowing how to identify them, but we shouldn't be so scared that we never go on a hike or somewhere new.

Yes, there are frightening things online: pornography, sexting, data breaches, grooming, and many more. But we must let data and facts, not fear, drive our parenting decisions.

Chapter 7
Gaming

WHEN mother of four Anna Dees describes her childhood, she remembers the times biking and playing at her friends' homes. The parents always knew where the kids were by looking out the window and seeing whose bikes were on the lawn. Now, the game Fortnite is the new "bikes on the lawn." With the COVID-19 pandemic, visiting homes wasn't an option, and Dees found that "Fortnite really has been the way that kids are connecting. They are literally playing with the kids next door or across the street . . . that's how they connect. They connect on Fortnite, not through cell phones. They just check Fortnite to see who's on."

As I'm writing this in late 2020, a second surge of the COVID-19 pandemic is hitting the world, and gaming has become even more popular, often serving as a social lifeline for many of our kids. The NPD Group, the largest market research company in the world, reported video game sales in North America up 34 percent in March 2020 from March 2019. Sales of video games and hardware reached a ten-year record high of $6.6 billion by July 2020, outpacing sales in books, movies, and television combined.

The influx of games into people's routines and homes in 2020 and 2021 may permanently adjust our perspectives. I know I've had my own feelings about games change this past year. I confessed in my previous book, *Becoming a Digital Parent: A Practical Guide to Help Families Navigate Technology*, some prior biases against gaming. While I was a gamer in childhood, as an adult I had come to see gaming as a time waster. I struggled to see the positives. But then my child got more into gaming, I talked to other gamers, conducted my own research on the topic, and in my book described how my feelings had evolved. I changed from a suspicious skeptic to a positive proponent of gaming.

While writing that book, I interviewed Professor Christopher Ferguson, a media researcher who focuses on gaming. I learned so much from him that I talked to him again for this book. He provides his outlook on gaming during COVID-19 and the future:

> It's been a remarkable boon for video games. But for all the talk that games are going to be a disaster for people, it didn't happen. Even the World Health Organization said, "if you need to play video games to stay inside go ahead and do it." It was a significant change in the narrative, everyone got on board that video games are good. They help people socialize when they otherwise can't . . . stay in touch with each other and it helps you stay inside and not run around and get COVID. The world didn't end. Our screen time as a culture skyrocketed and it's still not the worst problem we have by any means . . . I think video games and screens are going to come out . . . . like Amazon . . . as one of the financial winners of 2020, and unlike Amazon, one of the good guys.

You may have more video games in your home after COVID-19. I certainly do. It's been a way I connect with my child. We have been playing JRPG, Japanese role-playing games, together. We go on quests, get invested in the characters, search for loot, and spend time discussing the game asking questions like, "Who's your favorite character?" "Where should we go next?" "How do we kill this boss?"

We sing along to the game songs, crack jokes, and cuddle. It's been a fulfilling and important way to bond.

Games have that power to connect. Multiple generations across multiple continents can all connect together. But there are concerns. This chapter will focus both on the positives and the concerns through the 3 Ms of Digital Parenting framework. It will share stats and stories for you to help create positive gaming norms in your home. Perhaps you'll be like me and find this chapter and your own experiences giving you a new outlook.

COVID-19 disconnected us from schools, workplaces, and our traditional places to socialize and interact. Games are certainly not a perfect substitute for those places, but they've done a pretty good job. Anna Dees found all four of her children stuck inside this spring and summer with friendships and social connections "taken away." But, she said, videos games and "Fortnite replaced that in a really meaningful way."

What Does the Research Say?

Research into video games has a complicated and media-saturated history. Fears about video game violence and other dangers have existed since the 1970s. In *Moral Combat: Why the War on Violent Video Games is Wrong*, psychology professors Christopher Ferguson and Patrick Markey describe the beginnings of those fears—with the 1975 arcade game Death Race. Death Race was an extremely simple game with only black-and-white colors and lines and dots. In the game, the player tries to run over stick figures to get points and is rewarded by hitting the stick figures with tinny screams. Dr. Gerald Driessen, who researched Death Race "became one of the first psychologists to publicly propose a link between violent video games and real-life violence when he suggested that the interactive nature of the game might cause a small proportion of the population to become violent when they got behind the wheels of real cars." Games have come a long way from black-and-white lines and dots with many more car games, most notably Grand Theft Auto (GTA).

Despite decades of time and dozens of games, Driessen's prediction of more pedestrians dying from being purposely hit by other drivers has not happened.

The book *Moral Combat* goes on to describe a potential reason for this fear and panic around video games:

> Very often when a new form of media or technology is released, society goes through a period of moral panic in which this media or technology is blamed for any number of social kills, whether real or merely perceived. These panics can be explained in large part by generation gaps in adopting new technology or media. The young are far more proficient at adapting to innovation than are the old. This can create a perception among older adults that they are losing control of the culture they helped shape.

Since Death Race there has been a cottage industry of click-bait media articles, questionable research, politicians, think tanks, and more that continue to share misinformation about violent video games. In 1986, two researchers published their findings about the Atari 2600 video game Missile Command and wrote in an article in the *Journal of Applied Social Psychology* that the game had "measurable consequences" for aggression in the child subjects. While the verdict in this article seems clear-cut, the research behind the author's conclusion is suspect. In the study, young people self-reported their feelings about the game by responding to questions/statements like, "I feel willful" or "The person running the study was not very courteous." How are these statements related to aggression? The game in question, Missile Command, had no blood or people, it was a rocket shooting white dots on a black screen.

Another issue with studies of video game aggression is that the feeling of frustration is similar to the feeling of aggression. If you're playing a difficult level and you get stuck, lost, you die, and have to start over—you will feel negatively. But those negative feelings aren't necessarily about wanting to hurt someone but rather that you can't progress in the game. Parents should also remember that there's a difference between an attitude and actual behavior. I share this analogy in my presentations with parents: I may have the knowledge not to eat too much sugar, I may have an attitude that sugar is not best for my body, but that doesn't necessarily mean that my behavior toward consuming sugar will change. Behavioral change is complicated and driven by a host of environmental, biological, and other factors. Just because your child yells at a screen, or feels frustrated playing a game, does not mean that they will actually perpetuate violence.

After that 1986 article, the research around violence in video games seems to have died down—until the mass shooting at Columbine High School in 1999. After that incident, the media jumped on the fact that the shooters played the "violent" video game Doom, as a reason for the shooting. The shooting was so shocking to America that parents, educators, politicians, and others seized on a reason, any reason, to explain what happened. They were scared. Parents were scared and that fear drove them to want answers.

Those fears can also drive people to irrational decisions. I was in high school when the Columbine shooting happened, and the administrators in my school reacted strongly. An assembly was called, and new rules were put in place. One of the rules was that students could not wear leather trench coats. (A rule banning trench coats was supposed to stop a school shooting?) This was because some media outlets had made a connection between the black trench coats worn by the shooters and those worn in the 1999 film *The Matrix*. A 2006 ABC News article wrote:

> When Eric Harris and Dylan Klebold attacked Columbine High School on April 20, 1999, killing thirteen people and themselves, investigators said the killers evoked Neo, Keanu Reeves's character in the Matrix. The two teens were known for wearing long black trench coats similar to the one "Neo"

wears in the film and calling themselves the trench coat mafia.

Other outlets and politicians spouted this theory, with no evidence, that *The Matrix* and video games contributed to the Columbine massacre.

As an adult, I can empathize with the school administrators who were likely under lots of pressure to do something, anything, to calm and reassure. But, as you can imagine, the rule backfired. Many of my fellow students started wearing their own black trench coats in protest. At first, teachers and the school administration tried to crack down on removing students who wore them, but as more students donned trench coats, the administrators must have realized that they couldn't kick out a high percentage of the grade—perhaps they also realized that the rule was well-meaning, but dumb.

Are we as parents also creating "dumb" rules around video games because of our fears? We may find, like my school administrators, that those rules may backfire on us. Rules with no rationale and motivated by fear can lessen respect and trust between parent and child. This happened in my high school when the "no trench coat rule" was made arbitrarily with no input and no understanding of prevention science. In response to that rule, the students viewed the administrators as out of touch, bullying, and, frankly, stupid. If you view someone as a bully or unintelligent, of course you will rebel against their rules.

Sometimes organizations also make hasty pronunciations. In 2005, the American Psychological Association (APA) put out a policy statement about video games saying, "Comprehensive analysis of violent interactive video game research suggests such exposure a.) increases aggressive behavior, b.) increases aggressive thoughts, c.) increases angry feelings, d.) decreases helpful behavior, and e.) increases physiological arousal."

Since then, research has not arisen in the last fifteen years to support that statement, so the APA has revised it. In a press release sent out in spring 2020, the APA wrote "There is insufficient scientific evidence to support a causal link between violent video games and violent behavior, according to an updated resolution adopted by the American Psychological Association." In their 2020 press release, the APA acknowledged that "violence is a complex social problem that likely stems from many factors . . . attributing violence to video gaming is not scientifically sound and draws attention away from other factors, such as a history of violence, which we know from the research is a major predictor of future violence."

As children in the 1970s, 1980s, and 1990s became parents, they might have remembered their parents' and the media's words about the dangers of video games—and realized those predictions have not come true. Video games are also not such a new form of media now, they are ubiquitous in households around the world. But despite a lack of research, the strong belief in a correlation between video games and violence persists. That narrative came up again in 2018–2019 after a rash of tragic school shootings. The story of connecting games to delinquent behaviors will probably never go away. Why it will never go away is not because there's evidence to support it, but because of our own human desire to understand. We want to clearly see a cause and effect. Uncertainty and nuance are uncomfortable. We want a black box to explain the situation.

Parents and caregivers should not worry that video games will cause violence and aggression. In fact, there's recent research out of Oxford University that reports higher levels of happiness from certain games. The researchers, instead of relying on self-reports, looked at game industry data from two all-age games. As reported in the *Guardian*, "the researchers hope the study will introduce a higher standard of evidence to discussions about the concept of video game addiction, or digital harms in general." Andrew Przybylski, the lead researcher, is quoted as saying:

You have really respected, important bodies, like the World Health Organization and the NHS allocating attention and resources to something that there's literally no good data on. And it's shocking to me, the reputational risk that everyone's taking, given the stakes. For them to turn around and be like, "hey, this thing that 95 percent of teenagers do? Yeah, that's addictive, no, we don't have any data," that makes no sense.

Gaming Trends

As mentioned, 2020 was a huge year for games, not just because of the increase in sales and players, but also because of new consoles and technology.

Here are some highlights of recent gaming trends:

- **Ray tracing**: As machine learning improved, graphics improved. Previously used for CGI in TV and movies, games are utilizing ray tracing to make hyperrealistic graphics. Ray tracing uses algorithms to understand the way light works in an environment. This huge upgrade is in the new generation of consoles.
- **Discord**: In 2020, the Discord social platform had a huge spike of growth and as of late 2020 there are over 100 million active users.
- **New consoles**: The PlayStation 5 and Xbox Series X and Series S came out in November 2020. It is rumored that a new Nintendo Switch will be released in 2021 or 2022.
- **5G technology**: The speed of 5G data transfer will open up new opportunities for mobile games in 2021 and beyond.
- **Personal Computer (PC) improvements**: The speed and compression powers of most PC processors in the last few years allow anyone to have console experiences on a PC. A few years ago, it was harder to play certain console high-frame-rate games on a regular PC. You would need to upgrade to a gaming-specific model with an expensive monitor. If you want to stream media or your child is deeply

into gaming or competitive eSports, upgrades are most likely needed, but your average gamer can have a great time on a normal PC or even a laptop.

2021 and 2022 will almost certainly continue to bring faster speeds, better graphics, and more users. But beyond the hardware and software, the way we play games has also changed.

Never before have we had so many generations playing video games. And companies know that, introducing popular "nostalgia" games that parents will be particularly excited about. Vintage arcade emulators, basically arcade games preloaded with hundreds of old classics, are available to put in a corner of your home, or on your lap. Console manufacturers are also bringing back old hits aimed at older Millennials and Gen Xers. Nintendo has their original Super NES Classic, there's the Atari Flashback, PlayStation Classic, and Sega Genesis Mini.

Perhaps you don't play games now, but you used to as a child. Playing retro and nostalgic games and devices can be a bonding experience between you and your child. In my home, my child and I enjoyed playing the original Super Mario Brothers and Legend of Zelda together. He learned quickly that old games are tough!

Game Play

The way games are played has shifted throughout the past decade. In the 1980s and 1990s, if you wanted to play a game with someone, you both needed to be in the same room playing the same console and most likely you were sitting on the floor close to the TV since the wires to the controllers only went so far. The Internet has since connected players together from around the world. You can now cross-save your game, saving it on one device and playing it on another.

Increasingly, gamers are cross-playing. Cross-platform play is when you play with other people across different platforms, like one person on a PlayStation and the other on a PC. Cross-play has given older and fading games a new audience and is creating more online communities. Part of this push to cross-play is because of the wild popularity of games like Fortnite. Initially, Sony, where Fortnite was played, did not want the game on other platforms, but now it's available on mobile devices, PC, Nintendo, Xbox, and more.

Cross-playing may grow, but it has big tech obstacles. Epic Games, who owns Fortnite, is currently engaged in a lawsuit with Apple. Apple takes a 30 percent cut from companies and developers who want their app on the App Store. Google also takes the same cut on Google Play. To avoid that fee, Epic Games requested players make a purchase through their portal, which breached the contract with Apple. This move pushed Apple to remove Fortnite from their iOS App Store in fall 2020. Epic Games sued Apple for antitrust violations, claiming that Apple had engaged in monopolistic practices. So far, the judge assigned to the case seems skeptical of Epic's argument. She said, "walled gardens have existed for decades. Nintendo has had a walled garden. Sony has had a walled garden. Microsoft has had a walled garden. What Apple's doing is not much different."

The idea of "walled gardens," platforms and spaces online that are private and create their own rules and policies, is an issue across the entire Internet. It raises questions such as, "Who gets to decide what speech is allowed and what is not?" and "Who is responsible for bad behavior on the platform?" The Internet is a disparate mix of fiefdoms governed by different authorities, companies, local policies, and whims of moderators and individuals. This can make it difficult to navigate and legislate. There is not necessarily one centralized authority a parent can go to and say "stop this" or "take this down." When issues do happen in a game, after talking to their child, a parent should contact the game manufacturer. If the issue happened on a console's online platform like Microsoft Live, Nintendo Switch Online, or PlayStation Plus, there are parental controls and contact information to look into. If a parent's concern is not addressed through those means, there are a few other options:

- Federal Trade Commission (FTC) has an online complaint form to report online fraud, scams, and bad business practices in the United States at ReportFraud.ftc.gov.
- National Center for Missing and Exploited Children (NCMEC) has a centralized CyberTipLine at CyberTipLine. org where parents or caregivers can report online grooming, child pornography, child sex trafficking, and/or unsolicited obscene materials sent to a child.
- No responses from the company? Use the media. Tweeting or linking to the company may get you a quicker response than using official contact forms. Bad publicity can get attention.

There are local jurisdictions that can assist with illegal or obscene activities as well. Perhaps cross-play will continue to grow, which is both a potential problem, and a chance for change. Walled gardens may protect the company rather than the consumer. If more people, particularly minors, are playing across multiple ecosystems, there would be more pressure and demand for better moderation and protections. But young people playing on these online platforms have increased exposure of cyberbullying, obscenity, and other harmful content. Cyberbullying in gaming will be discussed later in this chapter.

eSports

Electronic sports, or eSports, are organized competitions using video games. Gaming has always had competitions. In the early days, it may have just been a showdown at the arcade, but with the growth of streaming and gaming in general in the 2010s, eSports exploded. The most popular types of eSports games are multiplayer online battle arenas, first person shooters, battle royales, or real-time strategy games. Esports are popular globally, particularly in China and South Korea. Statista estimates that by 2023 there will be 646 million viewers of eSports worldwide, "a large increase from the 395 million in 2018."

Esports is big business, and the top players can make millions. The top three players in 2019 made more than $3 million each. Collectively, the top ten eSports earners made more than $25 million in 2019, all with Dota 2 and Fortnite. Young people may follow these players and look at the numbers and decide that they want to get into eSports. This may alarm parents, who see the hours behind a screen and get concerned that something's wrong.

Video game researcher Christopher Ferguson advises parents to look at video gaming like other hobbies or interests. "If you take the DSM's link of Internet Gaming Disorder, and you take out gaming and you put in something like soccer, they inadvertently come out as addicted. They have all the same symptoms: it relaxes them to play their sport, they think about their sport when they're not playing it, they've given up other activities to do the thing." Think about something you really enjoy. For me, it's reading. If the DSM-V, the "Bible" used by psychologists, therapists, and psychiatrists to diagnose individuals, had a "reading disorder," surely I would have that label. Reading relaxes me, I stay up too late reading, I think about what book I want to read next, and I don't do other activities I could do because I'd rather be behind a book.

Why do we treat books, or sports, or music, or any other hobby differently than gaming? And doesn't any activity require a lot of hours to excel? "Essentially to get really good at an activity you'll find that it does require a certain degree of what we're choosing to call addictiveness," said Ferguson. "We can talk about piano addiction if we really wish to, but that's valued in a different way than gaming. That's the bigger issue, the different value systems of gaming."

In this book, I've asked parents to examine their own norms and values in their home. Do we value non-screen activities because they are more familiar and "how it was when we were kids"? Do we dismiss our child's interests online because we don't share the same interests? Although it is true that there can be excess in any activity, are we treating video gaming differently?

Christopher Ferguson recounts a question from parents about their adult child's interest in eSports:

> I remember getting an email from a parent of an adult son who wanted to be an eSports athlete. The son wanted to drop out, and of course, the parent was freaking out. The parent was very nice and reasonable but there was an element of "this is our kid, he's very smart, he's thrown us all for a loop, we're worried about addiction, but on the other hand he really wants to do it." I said, "come up with a plan, you can do this for a year and you need to show us some degree of success . . . have a concrete time period, you give it x number of years . . . if you can't support yourself after x number of years consider it's not working out and go back to university." I think that's what they did, the compromise to make that work.

This is a story about a college student, not a middle schooler who doesn't have the option of dropping out of school. However, Ferguson makes the point to strike a balance between supporting your child's dreams, and having your child be able to function and support themselves in the real world. "It's tough for parents," Ferguson acknowledges. "You don't want to be the one who ruins their kid's dream, on the other hand you don't want your kid doing something dumb." Esports is a new and growing field that parents may not know exists. Parents may not even know it's a real thing. Ferguson says it's "like 'Dad, I want to be a cartoon character' and the parent saying, 'Is that a thing?'"

Professor Ferguson gives these suggestions to parents whose children are interested in eSports:

- **Treat it like going into any sport**. "You're unlikely to get it, have a plan B. I would say the same thing for anyone who wants to be in the NFL."
- **Make sure their physical, social, and emotional health is taken care of**. "The same kind of general rules apply to any parent whose kid is gaming at all," Ferguson said. "They're getting their academics done, they're getting adequate sleep, they're essentially happy, and they're getting physical exercise as well."
- **Evaluate your own values on gaming**. Are you treating playing video games differently than other sports? Are you making allowances in non-gaming activities that may affect your child's physical, social, and emotional welfare? "We judge football differently than how we judge video games," Ferguson said. "Becoming an athlete is worthwhile but being a video game player is not worthwhile."

Model

Young children are engaging in social games more than ever before. A 2020 Common Sense Media survey report found that, since 2011, children aged eight and below shifted their game use from a computer or console to a mobile phone. Overall, the time young children spend on games has remained steady, it's the platforms that have changed. The youngest children, two and below, play virtually no digital games. This makes sense since they do not have the verbal or motor skills to properly play. However, as children reach elementary school age, both the time spent gaming and the gender gap of game play increases. Young boys average twice as much gaming time as girls, according to the report. This may be in part because girls are not encouraged to play games, they simply might not like them as much, or the creators of games don't make as much content that appeals to girls.

How are we modeling healthy gaming behavior for young children? Children are playing games, particularly on smartphones, but what are the best games? What should they be playing? And what should parents watch out for in games at these ages?

Setting Boundaries

In a 2020 survey by Common Sense Media, parents of young children were asked if it was difficult to get their child to stop using media when asked. Forty percent of respondents said that they agreed it was difficult. I can't blame children for protesting when media is taken away—I know I would protest if you took away something that I was enjoying. But part of growing up and being successful at life is self-regulating. One skill for the first M, self-regulation, is developed in the early years. When parents set boundaries around games and other media at home, it can help children self-regulate now and set their own boundaries later.

Technology has dissolved some of the boundaries between work/ school and home. It's ever-present, and particularly affects young children as they start school and establish new routines. I had a family media consultation with a mother of several school-age children who wanted help setting boundaries, particularly during those after-school hours. In our conversation, we identified tech- and non-tech solutions to this issue.

Some tech solutions are:

- **Lock down browsers**. There are browser plug-ins that limit the number of tabs that can be pulled up at any time.
- **Use a timer and music**. If children begin to associate a time, song, and place for work, they more easily get into the rhythm. Play music and have certain activities in specific places in the home. For example, homework could be done at a particular table with a specific playlist.
- **Lock and limit**. For one of Anna Dees's children who struggles with boundaries, she locks down his chrome book. "He has to do certain things and comes to me. He has to earn time." There are different apps and browser plug-ins with parental controls that can lock and limit. While these

tools are not as effective with teens, they can help young children. "I have learned a lot on these parental control pieces," Dees said.

Some non-tech solutions are:

- **Games are not allowed until dinner/homework/activities are done**. Games can be an incentive for children to finish their work.
- **Have a dedicated, consistent time for work**. For my son, we found that games were such an incentive that he was rushing through homework. One quarter of his grades fell because he was skipping homework questions or answering them sloppily. We then instituted a non-negotiable homework time that would decrease if his grades improved. When he knew that no matter how much homework he had, or how quickly he worked, the time remained the same, he focused more.

What works for one family may not work for yours. But one constant is constancy. When children know what to expect day in, day out, they are more likely to respect boundaries and follow rules.

Concerns with Gaming for Young Children

When evaluating gaming and children under eight years of age, there are certain things parents should be aware of. Young children are at a very important place developmentally, and games have the opportunity to help or hinder that natural developmental process. When making the decision to allow games or what games to play, parents should consider two big issues: safety and physical activity.

Online Safety

While games may have ratings and age recommendations, there's no foolproof method to separate young children from teens and adults on multiplayer online games. This means young children, who are lacking context for the world and still learning to communicate, may be exposed to foul language, hate speech, sexual content, and, although unlikely, could be exposed to grooming and other predatory behaviors. In addition, it's developmentally normal for children to look up to older peers. A kindergartener thinks second graders are brilliant, and the second grader wants to be like the fifth graders in their school. Dees describes this issue with her younger son, A:

> One of the other challenges is that A is six and pretty advanced himself and he wants to be with the bigger kids. We kind of need the bigger kids to keep track of him. He's been indoctrinated with video games earlier than the others . . . so he's learning some social things that I would not necessarily want him to see. He's witnessed bullying in some instances.

To help keep young children safe in online games, parents should:

- **Find games that are single-player**. Some of the safety concerns of games involve playing with others. For young children, restrict them to only playing with friends or family that they know in real life. Consider solo-modes or creative mode on Minecraft or other games that don't allow interactions with other users.
- **Talk to older siblings**. Young children may be inadvertently exposed to inappropriate content from their older siblings. Make sure older siblings know what they can and can't do or say around their little brothers or sisters.
- **Stay offline**. Find a mobile game that can be played offline, or a console game that doesn't connect to the Internet. This can restrict outside content for the game.
- **Play games with your child**. This goes for all ages, but particularly young children. Play games with your kid and talk to them about what they see.

Discord is a social platform where people can create private servers to stream, chat, and share pictures, videos, and more. It was originally set up for gamers, although any topic can be found on one of its servers. Since the COVID-19 pandemic in 2020, Discord had a massive spike in users. It also had a massive spike in reports of harassment. That harassment includes bullying, posting exploitative content, hacking, and sharing nonconsensual pornography.

Discord is recommended for older users, but young children may want to join to be part of the discussion on popular games like Fortnite, or to talk with their friends. In fact, 2020 research from the Cyberbullying Research Center found a growing number of tweens using Discord, 8.1 percent as of October 2020.

One positive of Discord is that parents can set up private, password-protected servers for their children to talk or stream with their friends. A negative, however, is the large public and open platforms where a young child may find themselves exposed to inappropriate content and adult strangers.

Physical Activity

Obesity in children has grown over the last generation. When someone's body mass index (BMI) is at or above the 95th percentile, they are considered obese, and at an increased risk for diabetes and other preventable diseases. The Centers for Disease Control (CDC) estimates that among children and teens between 2–19 years old, about 19 percent are obese. The CDC recommends preschool-aged children "should be physically active throughout the day" and older children, ages 6–17, should have at least one hour or more of daily "moderate-to-vigorous intense physical activity." Young children in particular need additional physical activity. While our sedentary lives behind screens are just one small part of the growth in obesity, we can all do better to move more. Video games can both encourage less movement—and more.

Compared to television, video gaming burns more calories. "Sedentary video game play involves more caloric expenditure than television viewing," according to a 2013 journal article in *New Directions for Child & Adolescent Development*. The article goes on to summarize new and growing research on "exergames" and mobile games that "have untapped promise to get youth to exercise and even lose weight." Some examples of those "exergames" include Pokémon Go, Wii Sports, Wii Fit, GoNoodle Games, and Sports Party.

Game Recommendations for Younger Children

For very young children, ages three and below, staying off digital games completely is a good developmental choice. As noted earlier, the transfer deficit for toddlers and younger means that they struggle with learning from screens, but when they reach preschool-age, games that can help with literacy and mobility are helpful. Children are learning letters and starting to write, which requires stronger and flexible hands. Games can help with that coordination.

Elizabeth Sarquis is the founder of the Global Gaming Initiative and has a background in child and adolescent development. Her organization works to help partners develop games that are fun, educational, and have a social impact. For children preschool-age up to eight, Sarquis recommends such games as:

- Minecraft
- Super Mario Maker
- Tetris
- Games that require coordination such as Mario Kart and Rocket League
- Games that require strategy such as chess, Pizza Maker, Overcooked!, and My Talking Tom

Sarquis also says that any game that introduces music to these ages "is a plus."

Whatever games you decide to play with your child, do your research. Not all games are created equal. Jon R. is a father of three. He says he's been "playing video games since before Oregon Trail" and now plays them with his children. When asked about gaming, Jon recommends:

> Parents need to take the time to look at the science and real studies. They need to learn about the specific games their kids want to play and talk to their kids. If they do that, they will have a better understanding that games aren't inherently bad or good. Just like movies, they are a form of entertainment. So, just like movies, TV, etc., parents need to be aware of what the kids are interested in and see if it is appropriate for them.

Manage

Dr. Patchin of the Cyberbullying Research Center worked with Cartoon Network in 2020 to look at tweens' behavior on social media and in gaming. Through that work, they found that 42.2 percent of tweens (described as 9–12-year-olds) had their own gaming console and 27.6 percent possessed a portable game player. Tweens are gaming, and younger tweens are more likely to have a gaming device rather than a smartphone. How can parents help manage their tween's gaming life? The first step is looking at media and games through the 3 Cs.

The 3 Cs and Gaming

Anna Dees is the mother of four children with varying abilities. She describes an experience with her neurodiverse child playing the controversial game Grand Theft Auto V (GTA). This action-adventure game has received criticism from parents due to its violent content, and it's been accused of sexism. But in her kid's situation, he was not affected by the content. Dees describes him as always having "this blur of reality and fiction."

Dees arrived home one day and saw her son's character sitting on a couch in a house in the game. "I said, what are you doing buddy?" and he said, "I just like watching the show that this guy's house has." Dees said, "My mom brain goes off, but in this context, it's harmless. In GTA, it's interesting. It's kind of like a way of role playing these social situations that we're all going to navigate at some point . . . but there's language and there's violence." For Dee's child, he spent most of his time playing GTA interacting and talking to characters . . . and watching TV on the TV in a game.

Parenting experts like senior researcher Michael Robb from Common Sense Media recommend using the three C's when evaluating content. It's a holistic approach that goes beyond ratings, screen time, or popularity to truly understand if the media is a good fit for the child.

- **First C: Child**
  - Examine the child's personality, interests, and hobbies.
- **Second C: Content**
  - Look at the content of the media. Is it well made? Does it have good reviews? Is there any content that may be scary or not age appropriate for children?
- **Third C: Context**
  - Where, when, and how is the media consumed? Is it designed to be played solo or with a friend/sibling? Is the media educational or entertaining? What device is the media played on?

When I teach digital parenting classes, I get asked about products for filtering or blocking apps. Parents want me to tell them the "best" way to prevent their children from seeing certain content. While I may give recommendations privately to parents, I don't do any product demonstrations in my classes. Products come and go, and I feel like parents may see them as a panacea to solve any technological problems—instead of doing the hard work of modeling, managing, and monitoring their children. But I also don't recommend specific products because those things only focus on one of the 3 Cs: content, and it's important to examine the context and the individual child as well.

Anna Dees has neurodiverse children; using a blanket strategy or product may not address the unique needs of her family. Grand Theft Auto may be inappropriate for some children because of content, but for Dees's son, the context, the way he plays, and the child, the way he sees the world, are different. If families are playing a game that may be rated for older children, but they do it together and discuss what they see, that context may be great, although the content might not be appropriate. For very young children, I do recommend some filters—because of context. Young children don't have the experience or background knowledge to understand what they're seeing. They engage in "magical" thinking. For a small child who believes in Santa Claus and monsters under the bed, how can they distinguish what's real and fake in a game?

Games and other types of media should be seen through a lens of the 3 Cs. Here's a hypothetical scenario with a fictitious tween:

Maria is twelve years old and just got her first phone. She uses her phone to talk with her friends, and recently her friends started playing the action game Among Us. Maria wants to download the game on her phone. Since getting the phone, Maria's grades have been slipping, she has missed some assignments, and turned others in late. Her parents are concerned that her homework is being neglected because of the phone, but they do observe that Maria is happy with her close-knit and communicative group of friends.

By breaking down the 3 Cs, Maria's caregivers can make a clearer decision on allowing/not allowing her to play the game. They can weigh the pros: the content isn't graphic, her friends are on it—with the cons: it may distract from homework and be time-consuming, she could be talking to strangers.

Table 7.1

3 Cs	Questions to ask	Good for Maria?
Child	Will the game Among Us appeal to Maria?	The game is well-reviewed and popular among Maria's age group and friends.
Content	What's the content of the game? What's the rating? Is the game diverse and representative of different groups of people? Do they play with strangers?	The game is rated 9 or 10+ and does have some mild violence and blood. If Maria plays with her friends, content may not be an issue, but if she plays with strangers, it could be an online safety issue.
Context	Is this an educational game? Where would Maria play it? When would Maria play it?	This isn't an educational game, but it does require strategy and communication. Maria would play it on her phone and with her friends.

Cyberbullying and Gaming

Gaming is sometimes a tween's first foray into online chatting. There is a blur between social media and gaming—I tell parents to think of gaming like another form of social media. Gaming is a communal sport, and while kids may not be playing against others, they are likely to be following others on streams, discussing games on Discord or other platforms, or following their favorite eSports stars or other gaming influencers. And since gaming is done collectively and with others, it poses a risk of increased cyberbullying.

According to Dr. Patchin and Cartoon Network's 2020 report on tween's online behavior, one in five tweens has experienced cyberbullying in some form. This can mean witnessing cyberbullying, being cyberbullied themselves, or bullying others (although the report found few tweens admitting to cyberbullying others).

Dr. Patchin and other researchers want it to be clear that although there is a connection between cyberbullying and gaming, when controlling for age, race, and sex in teens, there's only a 5 percent variation. This means, and is backed up by research by Dr. Christopher

Ferguson, that gaming in and of itself does not mean someone will be a victim or perpetrator of cyberbullying. In a blog post written by Dr. Patchin about his findings, he says "my review leads me to believe that there is a connection between gaming and deviance (and bullying behaviors specifically), but that influence is likely relatively small and mediated by many other factors (family, school, personal traits)—variables not included in our data." Patchin's statement goes back to the principle of prevention science—there are many risk factors and reasons *why* people do what they do. We cannot pinpoint one clear reason for behavior.

Patchin did narrow down a few reasons for why gamers cyberbully others:

- **Multiplayer games**: In games that include first-person shooters and battles, there are more reports of cyberbullying.
- **Hours a week played**: Young people who play less than two hours a day are much less likely than those who play more to have cyberbullied others.

If your child is playing more hours of games, it means there are more opportunities to witness, be a victim of, or a perpetrator of cyberbullying. The 2020 report also found a connection between bullying at school and cyberbullying. The report reads "93 percent of those who experienced cyberbullying also experienced bullying at school and 26 percent of those who have been bullied at school have been bullied online." If your child is having difficulties with peers at school, it's very likely that those troubles are online as well. Understanding your child's relationships and experiences in real life can help you protect them online.

How can parents help their tweens with cyberbullying?

- **First, help your tween know how to report, mute, block, filter, and control the settings in the apps and games they use.** The 2020 Cyberbullying Research Center found that

30 percent of tweens stopped cyberbullying by reporting it to the website or app, but that almost the same amount, 27 percent, did not know how to report cyberbullying incidents.

- **Encourage your child to help intervene with their peers.** While children should not be told to dive into the fray or do something that they feel uncomfortable with, they can anonymously report cyberbullying by taking a screenshot of the incident and reporting it. They can also personally message the victim and tell them something positive or say that they are there for them.
- **Tell your tween to save any records of cyberbullying.** This can include taking a screenshot, not deleting texts/emails, or taking a photo.

Game Recommendations for Ages 8–12

Children these ages, like the fictional Maria, are drawn toward their peers. They need social contact and connections, while still having accounts managed and guardrails in place. At these ages, you can take the Minecraft game out of creative mode into survival mode with friends. You can have your child get off their individual island in Animal Crossing to visit a friend or use the Safe Chat option in Roblox and use the multiplayer split-screen in Rocket League. Parents should still watch closely and manage passwords and accounts but allow more room for them to talk and connect with others in games.

Elizabeth Sarquis, founder of the Global Gaming Initiative, has game recommendations for ages 8–12:

- Minecraft (but now allow more freedom to play with others)
- Crossy Road
- Piano app by Yokee
- Logic and puzzle games such as Logic Master, Super Mario Maker 2, The Last Campfire, Untitled Goose Game, Wordscapes

When choosing a game for tweens, or any age, here are some questions you can ask when picking out a game. These are also questions that reinforce the 3 Cs mindset: child, content, and context.

- What is the game's rating?
- Does my child have time to play this game?
- Why does my child want to play this game? What are their reasons?
- Does it have microtransactions? If so, can I turn off purchases?
- Is this a game my child will play on mobile? Or another device?
- Does the game have access to the Internet?
- What are the game mechanics?
- Is this a game that is sedentary or has movement?
- Can this game be played as a family? Or is it a solo game?
- Does this game appeal to my child's interest?
- Will my child be talking with others through the game?
- How long is the game? Does it have an end?

When asking these questions, make sure you aren't imposing values, but rather reinforcing the positive norms in your home. A couple of important questions you should ask are:

- Is gaming in the home actually a problem?
- Or is it just a problem for you?

Perhaps your issue with gaming is that your child is not following in your footsteps. I know that I sometimes push my own desires on my son. I played piano growing up, taught it, loved it, and now have a piano in my living room. I've tried multiple times to get him interested, gently pressured, bribed—but he simply isn't into it. I admit I've been frustrated with his refusal—but that frustration comes from a good place. I want my child to be happy, and my faulty thought process goes like, *Well, piano makes me happy, so it should make him happy, too.* But of course, children are unique and have their own interests and those interests may be games.

Monitor

Monitoring your teen with gaming means taking that observational and mentorship role. Adolescents are increasingly independent with jobs, friends, and hobbies all outside the home, but gaming can be a place to come together. Jon R. discusses gaming with his teenagers:

> Now that my kids are older and enjoy playing, it is a way we can share an experience. We don't play many games together, but when we do, it can be really fun. You get to see their excitement when they beat me or just finish some puzzle. It has become a bonding experience, both while playing and after, just talking about them.

Gaming has positives and pitfalls. Some of those pitfalls for younger children, sedentary behavior and online safety, are also relevant to teens. But this section will address one looming trap where parents can play a key mentorship role: digital commerce.

Digital Commerce: Microtransactions in Gaming

Digital commerce, or any commercial transactions online, are a concept I reinforce as part of the third M of digital parenting. Young people are producers, buyers, sellers, and targets in the online ecosystem—and many of those digital commerce transactions start with gaming.

This has been something that has come up in Jon R.'s family with mobile gaming specifically. "The problem with mobile games is that they show way too many ads, the game itself usually isn't that good. Luckily, the Android play store has to have a credit card on file to buy things, so if you don't tie one to the account, you don't have to worry about charges." But many parents *do* tie credit cards to an account, or a mischievous young person can easily find a card in a purse. In one digital parenting class I taught, a mother asked me how her child was making all of these purchases without having her credit card. I told her that her kid did not need the physical card to make purchases, only the number. She was not happy to find that out.

Young people can get themselves in trouble with online gaming purchases. When a child turns eighteen, they may still be in high school, and at home, but legally they can apply for a credit card. While the Fed has tightened rules on credit cards for young adults, many can still get one. M, whose interview is featured in Chapter 8 on page 167, experienced this as a twenty-something young adult. He started playing GrandBlue Fantasy (GBF), a mobile role-playing game from Japan. GBF was a free-to-play game, although as M describes it, "at the time and probably still now, it has one of the most friendly free-to play models . . . when it comes to the grand scheme of predatory games, GrandBlue Fantasy is low on the predatory chart."

M describes GBF this way, despite getting sucked into what is called a "gacha," basically, a loot box. "You do a pull like a slot machine," he said. "You can do pulls anytime and get certain characters or weapons. There are certain characters that are rare and super cool." But then GBF, and other games like it, add this concept of "banners." A banner is a short window where the likelihood of winning rare characters or items increases. Other games employ this type of urgency tactic. For example, the popular mobile game Plants vs. Zombies, which does promotions for rare flowers, or the game Animal Crossing, in which certain items appear during the holidays.

M describes these banners as what "draws people in the most. You get excited, 'oh that new upcoming banner will help out my team,' and then you mentally prepare yourself to spend a ton of money in that short period." Through his short, four-month time playing GBF, M spent about $4,000. A friend of his spent more, almost $16,000, in just five months. He said that he felt FOMO (fear of missing out) and that he played the game too much. "It can be dangerous," he said. "You can sacrifice things. You can put it on a credit card since you have such a short amount of time to pull from that specific banner."

GrandBlue Fantasy is infamous because it actually contributed to changing law in Japan. "I remember hearing stories of people losing their mortgages because they were trying to get a character," M said. "That forced Japan to create a new law, so the game changed two things—they had to be transparent about the chance of you getting the thing" and GBF now allows players to buy the character if they spend a certain amount on pulls.

Despite spending thousands of dollars on GBF, M says other free-to-play games are worse. "I know there are some games, especially empire-building games like Clash of Clans, where what you pay for is to go faster. I feel like that's way more nefarious because, with a lot of those, if you're really into the game, you can't just sit there and do nothing for x amount of hours, so you start paying for the quicker construction of things."

What M experienced was the dark side of microtransactions: loot boxes. Microtransactions are any financial transaction in game play to enhance the experience. For example, you can spend real money to get tokens/gold or other fake digital monies to buy items in the game. These items can be anything from more Poké balls in Pokémon Go, to "skins" in Fortnite (a change in decoration or costumes). Microtransactions are not inherently bad, but parents do need to help their children understand budgeting and saving for what they really want. Perhaps a teen wants a new skin for their game, but they also are saving up for a car. Parents can remind their teen that more microtransactions means they're less likely to reach their big goal, the car.

Loot boxes are a type of microtransaction. Dr. Christopher Ferguson describes them:

You would pay a small amount of money, a dollar or two dollars, like a Christmas present, and you wouldn't know what was in the box. It would add this thrilling element. You get the box and the thing in the box would be a piece of junk or something really, really good. People get more concerned with that and it adds that sort of gambling-ish sort of element.

Ferguson makes the point that the idea behind loot boxes can be found in other toys: collectible cards, LEGO characters, those surprise eggs. Loot boxes are similar because "you don't know what you're going to get," but he adds, "the difference is of course with games you can do it over and over again . . . with LEGO characters they probably have only so many in the store."

The gaming industry is competitive with high overhead. Microtransactions have been a newish way for them to still offer their games at a cost for consumers. Developers, particularly with free-to-play or "freemium" games, rely on microtransactions to recoup their development costs and make money. But free games can definitely bring in revenue—just look at the billion dollars plus revenue of Fortnite.

Parents should have conversations about "freemium" or "free-to-play" games and create a gaming budget. Children may not understand the game's mechanics and that what seems free is not actually free. Teens may not fully grasp how they are being targeted and marketed to by large corporations. But, like in M's story, even adults can get sucked into these types of games. Young people, who are still developing self-regulation skills as their brains develop, are even more vulnerable. Ferguson recommends, "parents are wise to keep control of the money stream. Talk about money and credit cards and buying virtual stuff you can't use in the real world."

Other advice for teaching principles of digital commerce and monitoring microtransactions includes:

- Create passkeys or require two-factor authentication to prevent unauthorized purchases.
- Monitor your own bank accounts for unfamiliar transactions.
- Create separate child accounts not linked to credit cards.

- Enable restrictions on iPhones and disallow in-app purchases on games. This can be done through a Screen Time setting.
- Some settings on devices allow for a one-time password entry. This means your child can make purchases after putting in the password once. Change parental controls to requiring passwords each time.
- Google Play allows you to require a password or authentication for purchases. The Google Play store automatically requires authentication for purchases of apps or games for ages twelve and under.
- Sign out of consoles and accounts if you are sharing them with your child. That can prevent them from logging into your account which may be linked to a credit card.
- Do not put any credit card information on children's accounts. Buy them a gift card or prepaid card instead.
- If your child does go wild with purchases you don't approve, you may be able to get a partial refund. Contact the app store and report the incident.

Self-Efficacy

All the monitoring and managing in the world can only do so much for adolescents. They are and should be making their own decisions about when and how much time and money they want to give to games. Teens must develop self-efficacy, the confidence to make their own decisions. They must be the ones to ultimately say, "I've played enough games today, time to study" or "I've spent too much money on this game, I should stop."

Parents can help with their teen's development of self-efficacy by monitoring but creating broader rules together. Work with your teen to set a budget or to discuss what they must do to earn money for microtransactions. Talk with your teen about what time games need to be powered down at night. In Jon R.'s case, he has "set specific 'screens off' hours . . . when they need to be working and when they can play." Jon and his wife do not tell the children specifically what they have to be doing, they can still choose what to occupy their time within those hours.

Beyond setting limits on what they can't do, encourage what they can do. As noted earlier, adolescents can make income and even careers based on gaming. They are part of the digital economy more than ever before. In 2019, a sixteen-year-old, Kyle Giersdorf, won three million dollars to become the world champion of Fortnite. A fifteen-year-old and fourteen-year-old also walked away with major prizes and money from that tournament. While the vast majority of adolescents will not be millionaires from gaming, the adage that gaming is simply a waste of time is no longer true. But to reach their goals, whether in gaming or balancing gaming with life, adolescents need the self-control and self-efficacy to both set limits and expand them to reach their dreams.

Game Recommendations for Teens

For teens, game recommendations are harder to suggest. Teens are developing their own identity and interests and are widely variable in what they may want to play. Elizabeth Sarquis does not have many specific recommendations. In response to this question, she said, "This is more challenging since at this age teens will determine what they like depending on what their friends are playing, and games are inherently social." Sarquis recommends that parents see games for adolescents as a way to broaden their ideas about the world. "Games are global, and the connections kids can make with other kids across country boundaries are amazing. They can learn about different cultures through music and game-play interactions." She does have a few recommendations on her list for this age cohort:

- Puzzle games such as Wordscapes and Words with Friends.
- Pokémon Go or other social games to play with friends.
- Open world games such as Minecraft, Roblox, and a more advanced version of Minecraft: Terraria.

- Khan Academy. Sarquis says, "Although Khan Academy isn't a game, it should be on every parent's list for learning tools."

What Makes a Good Gamer?

In early 2020, experts from around the United States came together at the World Economic Forum for Raising Good Gamers. This workshop examined the impact of gaming on young people, particularly around bias and other systemic cultural issues. A report from this discussion acknowledged the nuances in gaming, stating, "Gaming culture can be exclusionary and discriminatory, reproducing and encoding systems of bias and inequity that pervade society as a whole." But also noting, "young gamers are having fun, learning from each other, and learning to be good citizens of gaming and online communities. They are able to transfer some of their skills and citizenship sensibility to other aspects of their lives."

This chapter covers some of those nuances—the ability of games to connect, but also to put children at higher risk for cyberbullying. The ability to make money or lose money. But as with other technologies, it's not gaming that's inherently the problem. The Raising Good Gamer's group writes, "Online aggression, hate, harassment, prejudice, and disruptive player behavior . . . has its root causes not in individual players or games, but in a system of interconnections, interactions, policies, patterns, and power dynamics. This system involves many stakeholders with different values and priorities who influence the system in various, interrelated ways."

When parents fearlessly address gaming in their homes, they should be aware of all the many influences that go into gaming behavior. The report lists some of those influences as:

- Streamers behaving inappropriately to maximize views.
- Games not fully controlling who plays their games despite age ratings.
- Younger players interacting with older and more toxic audiences in games.

- Lack of public access to data from game companies on potential harms in platforms.
- Lack of human moderation in games.
- Systemic bias in game design.

Parents may not be able to control all of these factors, but they can reinforce their own values and priorities with their children. And they can educate their children on these nuances and the systems of marketing, design, and psychology used to create the games they love. I'm more aware of these issues as a parent, yet still overcame my own bias and perceptions to see the value in gaming.

Chapter 8
Online Communication and Media Literacy

As I write this chapter, it feels like America and the wider world have been gripped by conspiracy theories and misinformation. There are elected officials who believe in QAnon, a wide-arching umbrella conspiracy. QAnon alleges that a small group of Satan-worshipping pedophiles who run a global child sex-trafficking ring are plotting against former President Donald Trump. Followers of Q await "The Storm," a day when the thousands of this cabal will be arrested. Misinformation about COVID-19 and mask wearing have brought protests minutes away from where I live. The modern day "flat-earthers" movement continues to grow with YouTube creators making videos viewed by millions. Anti-vaccination beliefs have grown and the World Health Organization identified these beliefs as one of the top global health threats of the 2020s.

When I teach digital parenting classes, I sometimes get asked what my biggest concerns are about technology. I say that it's not what other parents typically fear, like Snapchat or the latest app, sexting, pornography, etc. My biggest concern for young people, and adults, is media literacy, sometimes referred to as information literacy. This term refers to the ability to identify different types of information and understand what they're saying. Media literacy encompasses vital skills such as:

- Critical thinking.
- Understanding the media's role in society's cultural values.
- Evaluating our own biases and perspectives.
- Reflecting on the effects of media on our moods and emotions.
- Finding and consuming credible information.
- Understanding the media's intents and motivations on us.
- Knowing the effects of technology, algorithms, and more on our interests and media choices.
- Clearly and respectfully sharing and articulating our points of view.

What keeps me ruminating on media literacy is the growth and glut of information and its real-life harms on individuals, families, society, and democracy. People have literally died from causes related to a lack of media literacy. This can mean death by medical misinformation, government policies made based on false claims, and in extreme examples, by shootings, attacks, and violence.

To me, the greater danger with lack of media literacy is more subtle and slow—the gradual decline of public trust in the institutions that bind us as citizens and humans. Pew Research reports that public trust in the US federal government has "hovered at near-record lows" for years. In 2020, just 20 percent of US adults say they trust the government in Washington to "do the right thing" just about always or most of the time. Another 2020 survey of more than 20,000 American adults from Gallup and Knight found similar pessimism and skepticism. It reported that the "vast majority of Americans (84 percent) say that, in general, the news media is 'critical,'" or "very important" to democracy.

Despite our belief in the critical importance of the media, there are increased numbers of people seeing bias. The Gallup poll found that "nearly three-quarters of Americans say they see too much bias in the reporting of news that is supposed to be objective as a 'major problem.'" Four in five Americans say that the spread of misinformation online is a "major problem" and they feel overwhelmed. Sometimes when people feel overwhelmed, they opt out and check out. The number of Americans removing themselves from the news landscape has increased. Gallup and Knight report that 17 percent of them have stopped paying attention to the news altogether.

I'm seeing this feeling of overwhelm in students, too. I've had high school students espouse flat-earth beliefs in the classroom. When I teach media literacy, students tell me that they refuse to read or watch the news. I get where they're coming from; some days I feel burdened by the type and amount of information thrown at me from all directions.

I also don't blame young people for following conspiracy theories or opting out; they've grown up in a different media environment than previous generations. Baby Boomers had three main news channels, CBS, NBC, and ABC. Until the 1980s, these "big three" dominated American news networks. And they were pretty similar. You knew if you watched one it would have reporting like on the other station. You could feel that the news was reliable. It wasn't until after the 1980s and into the 1990s that twenty-four-hour news and cable networks started taking over the airwaves.

Young people, particularly teens, are getting their news more and more from social media. A 2019 Common Sense Media survey found that more than half get news a few times a week from Instagram, Facebook, and Twitter, and 50 percent get news from YouTube. Instead of curated and edited sources, or the reliable big three, they read a newsfeed. While mainstream news has accounts on all social media channels, adolescents are increasingly turning to celebrities and influencers rather than from news organizations.

Young people are bombarded with information from peers, feeds, influencers, videos, and more. They may feel like their parents, tired and beleaguered. Despite those feelings, the answer is not to shut down and opt out, but to step up. When we fall into nihilism and distrust, we are more susceptible to charismatic or strongman figures who do not have our best interests at heart. When we don't believe anything, someone *else* will give us something to believe in. "Media literacy *is* safety," said youth online advocate Anne Collier. "It protects us from being manipulated."

This chapter will discuss media literacy and online communication and the potential harms of online echo chambers, conspiracy theories, and misinformation. But it will also cover ways that parents can help. Being able to navigate and communicate online is a vital skill, not just for a career, but for being a participating citizen. As Collier adds, "you can't be a citizen without being an informed citizen."

Conspiracy Theories

Dr. Kristy Roschke is the managing news director of Arizona State University's NewsCo/Lab. She has taught media literacy to high school and college students and has experienced personally the pull of misinformation and conspiracy theories. When she was a new mom, she got pulled into a misinformation rabbit hole from online mom groups. "I've seen this in moms' groups that become anti-vaccine groups. You're a new mom and you find this group of people who are going through the same thing. It can feel very comforting and then you're ready to embrace that." Being a new mom is stressful; you may be isolated and wondering what you're supposed to be doing. You go online to seek advice and support, but you may find something else. Roschke said that when you find a group, it can be comforting and uplifting, and you let your guard down. You stop asking 'who are these people I should be trusting?' She said, "Soon, this mom in my group becomes more trustworthy than a doctor who wants to put a needle in my child's arm. It's a sense of community in the group—you go from being objective and at arm's length to saying 'oh, this is the thing.'" Roschke added, "There were definitely times when I was reading things where I'm like, 'this doesn't seem right but I'm willing.'"

Conspiracy theories and misinformation are tantalizing topics to people who may be feeling isolated like Roschke was, confused, or simply curious. These groups offer a clear black-and=white picture of the situation. They also provide support, conversation, comfort, community, and friendship. Dr. Roschke is an expert on media literacy and teaches journalism, but even she found the pull of misinformation strong. People who label those who share or believe in misinformation and conspiracy theories as "crazy" or "stupid" are not understanding the situation. By dismissing the individuals who believe, we isolate them even more and can entrench them further into harmful beliefs.

Why do people believe conspiracy theories? Dr. Whitney Phillips, a professor of communications at Syracuse University wrote for WIRED about the concept of "memetic frameworks" related to the QAnon conspiracy:

> Everyone, regardless of their politics, has a set of deep memetic frames. We feel these frames in our bones. They shape what we know, what we see, and what we're willing to accept as evidence. In the context of conspiracy theories, deep memetic frames establish the identity of the bad "them," as opposed to the valiant "us," and prescribe what can or should be done in response. QAnon and deep-state theories don't magically transform nonbelievers into believers; they're not viral in that sense. People are drawn to these theories, instead, because the narratives line up with their deep memetic frames. QAnon and the deep state feel familiar for those already inclined to believe.

While the definition of a meme can vary from discipline to discipline, it's helpful to think of it as cultural information that is easily passed to many. Memes can shape mindsets, behaviors, and actions of social groups. Memes are not simply funny images; they're shareable and easily imitated ideas. They're a tool often used in online echo chambers or toxic communities. A meme can be like a knowing wink or a password; if you get it, you're *in*.

Memetic frames are like digital identities. You may see this online in profile descriptions like "I'm a dog-person," "My kids are everything," "DC superfan," or "Outdoorsy." When I teach young people about memes and echo chambers, I use the word "bubble." I ask them, "What are your bubbles?" This can mean anything from a favorite food or sports team to a religion. We all have bubbles, and those bubbles, or frameworks, are easily deciphered by technology.

When we log in, our memetic frame goes with us, and algorithms know it. When we search for specific phrases, join certain online groups, click on ads, purchase items, all of these actions are logged and reinforced. If you watch a YouTube video related to a conspiracy, YouTube's algorithm may suggest more. If you are in a Facebook group with someone who is part of conspiracy Facebook groups, your algorithm will suggest the same groups as that other member. If you search for information on a conspiracy theory, Google will tailor its search results to your past searches.

Phillips describes what happens to people who get pulled into conspiracy theories online. "When users begin seeking out more information about conspiracies on more sites, and all that information is lining up, they end up subject to a media-wraparound effect." Algorithms give us information not based on facts, but on engagement and views. Google does not care about media literacy, only about advertising dollars. When someone keeps running into the same information online, they may assume that they've discovered some hidden truth. Or they may perceive that everyone believes in the conspiracy, rather than just a fringe group. At this point, coming at the belief directly, trying to debunk it, can do more harm than good.

Social media reinforces conspiracy theories. It amplifies voices. This is often a wonderful gift—technology can provide platforms to the marginalized or others who have been left out. It can diversify and democratize. But social media can also isolate and balkanize.

Christopher Ferguson, a media researcher, talks about the ability of social media to broadcast fringe beliefs:

> There's an argument that Twitter and other modalities like Facebook have had an unintended malicious influence on amplifying extreme voices. People who are . . . in the 5 percent category on the far right or far left . . . now have enormous influence where in any other rational, sane society they would not. Those voices are being amplified on social media. They get more attention than 90 percent of people in the middle.

Ferguson went on to describe a situation where he wrote on Twitter, "I can see the arguments on both sides of the abortion debate," and was labeled from those who were for and against abortion. He did not get nuanced debate to his Tweet. "There's an interesting argument that social media didn't cause this," he said. "These trends on both the left and the right have been there for some decades. But . . . social media allows for these more niche views to become amplified and because those people are so invested, they are very aggressive about it."

What can parents do if their children go down the conspiracy theory rabbit hole? Dr. Kristy Roschke has several recommendations:

- **Have healthy boundaries around media use**. This can mean limits on screen time so that your child has a balance of real-life and online time.
- **Have an open dialogue with your kids about all kinds of things**. Roschke recommends an attitude of "let's talk about the things we see and talk about." This can mean discussing the news as a family and not shying away from controversial topics.
- **Creative a normative culture in the family**. If children hear their parents espouse fringe beliefs, they are more likely to pick up on them.

"Once they're in the rabbit hole, and it can happen quickly, I think what I would say is have those conversations about who's telling you what and why," Roschke advises. She suggests talking about the feelings and emotions that drive someone to look at the misinformation. Parents can ask, "Tell me what this conspiracy theorist is telling you and why you think that's right?" Ask open-ended questions and ask *them* to tell you what the conspiracy theory says. Try to get them to articulate it and say it out loud.

Roschke also recommends talking to them about their beliefs or bubbles without shame. She says:

> You can't make them feel stupid. You can't make them feel crazy. You can't make them feel like they don't know what they're talking about. Presenting them a bunch of facts and calling them dumb is not going to help. What I've found is that I think there are people that get down these rabbit holes that buy into this amorphous idea of a conspiracy. But when you actually get down to the facts that they are finding, then you can find a claim.

A claim can be a specific assertion of the theory. In the case of QAnon, instead of "a global group of elites are pedophiles" you address "children being sold in pricey cabinets." One claim is vague and amorphous, the other more tangible and quantifiable. Address specific claims, gently and with open-ended questions, one by one. It's a slow process and probably not as satisfying as saying "you're crazy if you think Q is real," but it's more effective.

Q is just the latest and largest of conspiracy theories; they've always been with us. In America's early days, fear of the Illuminati conspiracy consumed many. And conspiracies regarding the Moon Landing, John F. Kennedy's assassination, and 9/11 are still talked about today. But unlike those early days, technology today has made conspiracy theories go viral. The need for conversations, patience, empathy, and media literacy are more important now than ever.

Online Echo Chambers and Hate Groups

M has been a 4chan user since its beginning in 2003. As described in Chapter 6 on page 93, 4chan is an anonymous forum that is the birthplace of some online conspiracy theories like QAnon, and the home of hate groups. I interviewed M to get an insider's view of 4chan. There are many media articles about the forum, but not many users speak out. 4chan is clearly on my Red Flag list and M acknowledges that he would not recommend any minors use it; but it has another side. I include their story to share an insider's view of trolling culture, the early Internet, online echo chambers, and generational and cultural divides between platforms.

M said 4chan wasn't always the way it is now, and still uses it periodically. Before 4chan, it was Something Awful, another anonymous forum site that still exists. "Something Awful was before then," M said. "If I remember correctly, the idea came out from conversations in Something Awful to start 4chan." He then goes on to describe Something Awful, whose philosophy has influenced 4chan:

> Something Awful was always a forum that, if I were to explain it, prided itself on expertise. Something Awful has all kinds of different sections with different categories and topics and what is most valued is knowing what you're talking about. They have a reputation for being assholes or dickheads because they will shut down and ban people they think are not knowledgeable. It's tough for a child to understand the culture, even for some adults it's hard, it's really harsh. Most people lurk. Anyone who speaks out, if they don't seem to know what they're talking about, will be easily attacked. It's just a culture, it's not ill-spirited, it's just that they really have this mentality of purging useless stuff.

That harsher culture and platform of categories moved to 4chan. "4chan is not for minors," M reiterates. It "is divided into subcategories that come from higher categories." Almost all posts are anonymous and users who create profiles are mocked. The hacker group "Anonymous" came from 4chan and this function. They adopted "Anonymous" because almost every user on 4chan is labeled Anonymous. Unlike other social media platforms, 4chan's posts are time sensitive. A post can quickly sink off the first page of the forum in minutes. 4chan is also not searchable or indexed, so images, controversial posts, and trolling can be quickly buried and lost.

When M is on 4chan now, he mostly stays on the Japanese culture board. He says that the Japanese culture, video game, interests, and creative categories may be "safe for minors to go to." However, M cautions that the other categories are just a click away.

4chan also has two Not Safe for Work (NSFW) categories, Miscellaneous and Adult. But what 4chan gets into the news for are the three categories of /b, /pol, or /r9k. "At the beginning of it, I wouldn't say there was a right or left ideology in 4chan," said M. "I've always been slightly to the left, but I love my Internet culture. It was all kinds of people. Over the last few years when I've decided to log back in it feels that the most inflammatory boards are the most right-leaning." M says that unfortunately those three most toxic boards have also become the most popular ones.

Here's a breakdown of those boards:

- **/b (Random):** This is the most popular image board that operates under a "no rule" policy, except for child pornography (CP) and minor visitors. Despite those bans, CP continues to be shared, and 4chan users began using the cartoon image of a brown bear, dubbed "Pedobear," to indicate that CP was shared.
- **/r9k (Robot 9001):** This is an image-only board that insists on original content. It's a popular place for incels (involuntary celibates) and the alt-right.
- **/pol (Politically Incorrect):** This board is a popular spot for hate groups and conspiracy theories. It's also part of the reason Donald Trump became so popular. "The 4channers never thought it would get like this," M reflects. "The /pol

people were joking about Trump because Trump was such a troll. People started throwing their support for him as trolls for a troll. They didn't think he would become elected. Listening to him call Mexicans rapists was funny at the time; we didn't think he would get elected."

Incels, or involuntary celibates, are part of an online subculture who claim that they cannot find romantic or sexual partners despite wanting one. The forums like on 4chan where incels gather are full of entitlement, self-loathing, resentment, and hatred toward women. The US nonprofit Southern Poverty Law Center said that they were "part of the online male supremacist ecosystem" and a "hate group." They have also been called a terrorist threat and are monitored by law enforcement. Six mass murders resulting in forty-four deaths have been committed by those who self-identify or interact with incel communities.

A related male supremacist online group is Red Pill. The term "Red Pill" is used in this community to refer to the "truths" that they claim about gender roles such as "marriage and monogamy do not benefit men" and the "world privileges women." The name Red Pill relates to the 1999 movie *The Matrix* where the protagonist Neo is asked to choose between a blue pill and red pill. The blue pill would lead him back to his normal life and the red pill would uncover the truths of the world. Members of the Red Pill movement typically mock and want to police female sexuality.

Other online male supremacist groups, referred to as the "manosphere," include Men Going Their Own Way (MGTOW) and Pick Up Artists (PUA). MGTOW followers prefer to separate themselves from women and, like other manosphere communities, overlap with white supremacists and the alt right.

Men's Rights Groups
The "Manosphere"

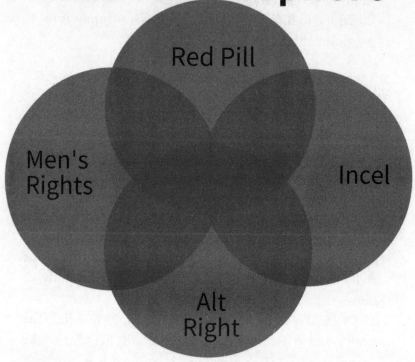

Trolling culture is huge on 4chan and, like M mentions, it has had a large impact on the world outside those anonymous boards. It's a controversial topic, and the line between a joke and harm is fuzzy and subjective. Trolling is also a difficult issue for parents who simultaneously want to protect their children from harm and prepare them for a sometimes-harsh world. Troll culture is alive and well on the Internet and in video games. M describes troll culture:

> When you're trolling someone, your goal at the end of the day is to inflame them. But you inflame them by making them believe something is true. You're trying to make people believe something ridiculous or believe that you yourself

believe something ridiculous in order to enrage them. That used to be fine because most people who were on the Internet had the thick skin to realize that "this person is trolling," but now there are a lot of people who believe that thing. I am a fan of trolling just like I'm a fan of jokes and comedy. But it's been hard not to realize when it comes to certain conspiracies, trolling is slightly to blame for it. I still don't blame the trolling, but I know that it's been a part that's contributed to things like Q happening.

Trolling intersects with hate speech. Online hate groups regularly use trolling, cyberbullying, doxing, or other tactics to target other individuals or groups they may disagree with. Hate speech is a powerful tool online because of the immediate emotional reaction. M describes its role in trolling. "Hate speech is a really easy way to troll someone. You say something so outrageous and if someone takes the bait you succeeded at trolling. It doesn't surprise me that hate speech and trolling go hand in hand." On 4chan, common ways to employ hate speech in trolling include anti-Semitic speech like "the Jews control the world" or homophobic speech like the use of the word "fag." If someone, particularly a young person with less online experience, is surrounded by this hate speech, it's no longer a joke. They may perceive that everyone feels that way and adopt some of those words, then beliefs, then actions.

Jokes can have major real-world harm. For example, Brendon Tarrant, the twenty-eight-year-old who killed forty-nine people at a massacre in two mosques in Christchurch, New Zealand, got inspiration from social media. Tarrant viewed the killing itself as a meme. He was immersed in white nationalist online forums. In his seventy-four-page manifesto, Tarrant recommended "edgy humor and memes," pointed to Jeb Bush, a presidential candidate in the 2016 election, as boring, and discussed how memes were effective in gaining support for Donald Trump.

These beliefs, like the online manosphere and forums like 4chan, and its even more harmful iteration 8kun (formerly 8chan), intersect and interact. Someone who has a white nationalist ideology most likely comes into "manosphere" groups which layer that ideology with misogyny. Reports about Tarrant and other shooters find a history of experience with these groups over a period of time. They get immersed in one subculture, then gradually move to even darker ones.

For most individuals, they never even visit these groups. They are not user-friendly; their graphics are a holdover from the early Internet. They can be confusing with many terms, images, and memes that are unfamiliar. Even if a young person visits 4chan, they may not stay for long or just visit the groups that appeal to their hobbies and interests. However, for a young person with preexisting conditions like mental illness or a sense of loneliness or trauma, these groups have a pull.

There is a generational gap between early Internet users and Generation Alpha and Gen Zers currently online. Gen Xers and older Millennials experienced a different Internet than their children. That Internet was less regulated, less corporate, and smaller. "The biggest thing about 4chan now I would say is the fact that more 'normies' reach it," M said. He goes on to say:

> Since its inception, 4chan has always been up on the jokes, the memes, the trolling, but there was a time in which everyone was in on the joke, and everyone understood it was a joke. But I noticed as mobile phones started becoming normalized that more people started joining that didn't get the joke and jokes became serious things like conspiracies and even /pol.

What Can Parents Do About Online Echo Chambers?

Younger users of the Internet may not be in on the "joke"—if it really is a joke. That line is blurry, and some users may excuse their behavior with "jokes" when there is an intent to harm. Young people, and older users, too, lack the context. They may not know the origination of the meme, the backstory of the phrase, or the history of the board/forum/group. They walk in as explorers from another land with its own set of culture and rules. M feels that their experience in the early Internet helped them develop a thicker skin and a radar for scams and jokes. He feels like the "normies" or passing travelers and minors are walking into a space they are unfamiliar with and misunderstanding the norms.

"I truly believe a joke, if it's funny, is mostly blameless," M said. "I mostly believe that the people who fall for it and think it's a real thing are people who can't take jokes and make it worse." But M acknowledges, "I cannot deny that the joke might be the small pebble that creates the avalanche. I'm of two minds of it. I will never say people should stop joking or trolling. But I also can't deny that it has been taken out of context and caused harm."

How can parents explain the context and the background of groups like these? "Parents need to know what 4chan is and 8kun and how easy it is to find it and what purpose it serves," Roschke said. The purpose for a teen may be loneliness, wanting something funny to pass the time, or seeking a community and companionship. In addition, the taboo of places like 4chan and 8kun can be appealing to a young person. These groups push back against the "normies" and are defiant, funny, and different. If a parent pushes back against a group, that can confirm that the parent/authority is "lame" and "boring" and just doesn't get it. Roschke said, "Trying to convince someone that the group is bad is a hard sell for someone who is deep into the group. They will say 'they said you were going to tell me this would be bad.' It's groupthink, it's cult mind."

Kids who are already vulnerable due to lack of experience, trouble at home, or issues with peers are more likely to get sucked into these online echo chambers, and wholeheartedly believe and adopt the "joke." Youth advocate Anne Collier said, "I remember a story in *The New York Times*," about a young person being radicalized. This 2019 story written by tech writer Kevin Roose was called "The Making of a YouTube Radical." Collier continues:

It was about a young man who lived in Kentucky with his grandparents . . . he was a very quiet young man, not particularly social, and a bit lonely and kind of casting about for what he wanted to do with his life. He went down a serious alt-right rabbit hole on YouTube. The recommendation engine turned up more and more extreme videos in that regard. He kind of got stuck in that rabbit hole for a while. But . . . he came back.

Collier goes on to say, "This young man figured out that this is a little bit weird. It seemed really one-sided. I think he got more and more uncomfortable with what he was reading and found his way out of that rabbit hole."

4chan user M gives this advice for parents about trolling culture and online forms: "Try to explain that it's trolling and that it's people joking around. Most of the people that started all these things didn't believe it themselves. I would try to educate them, show them the truth about things, and explain it to them." If young people start believing that everyone who makes a joke or meme truly believes what they are saying, they will get a distorted view of reality. It also makes things like racism and sexism more normalized. M adds, "Don't believe what you see online. The Internet is a great source of information, but as time goes on, I've noticed that the percentage of things that are accurate and true online gets lower and lower. You have to know your sources. As much as I love 4chan, it's not the trusted source for anything."

To summarize, some suggestions for parents who may have children dipping their toes or even diving into online echo chambers like 4chan include:

- **Watch for risk factors**. Monitor your child more after a breakup, divorce, death of a friend or family member, or other events in their life that may put them in a particularly vulnerable state.

- **Discuss context**. Look on sites like "Know your Meme" to understand where things come from. Most children, like your child, do not know where these memes originated, and they may be less likely to share or like certain images if they know their history.
- **Don't generalize or dramatize**. If you immediately ban and lecture and push back against some of these online groups, they may become even more taboo and alluring to your child. Monitor their usage, perhaps even sit down with them and look. Ask open-ended questions about beliefs. Address a "joke" with another "joke."
- **Teach media literacy**. Read on for more suggestions about encouraging media literacy.

Media Literacy Education

I was a librarian for about a decade, and I continue to write, train, and consult librarians. I took classes in media literacy in library school and would train patrons and students on how to find information. In those days, it was different. Information was harder to find; you had to dig deeper, look into specialized databases, and I would use Boolean logic to narrow down the search. Pages of curated links were more common, instead of the now ubiquitous magnifying glass in the corner of most websites.

I remember in the early days of being a librarian, patrons were more patient with a search. They expected it to take a little longer to find something. By the time I left librarianship to start Digital Respons-Ability, that patience was gone. They cared less about the source than the answer. They didn't want multiple sources as an answer, but one. They didn't care as much about the expensive databases the libraries used, or peer-reviewed journals. Patrons were used to getting their information instantly.

It's wonderful that we have such information at our fingertips now. We can find things quicker with less effort. But there's another side to that. While we have a greater quantity of information, we haven't necessarily increased the quality. And our habits of instant searching and answers have made us less likely to do the hard mental work of searching, identifying, and evaluating. While Americans report that they are more skeptical of news, this skepticism hasn't resulted in them using paid databases or adjusting their search strategies.

Finding reliable and unbiased information and media feels out of control to many people. They feel overwhelmed so stop trying. I was taught as a librarian that we are in control, that we can find accurate information and educate others to seize control of their own searching. I still believe that and continue teaching it to my students.

Fake News

One media literacy lesson I teach teenagers is about fake news. They've all heard the term but may not understand it. They also may not understand the different types of manipulation online. There is not just one type of fake news, and when we lump it all into one category, we miss the motivations and manipulations behind each type. There are four major categories under the umbrella of fake news:

- **Satire**: For young children, this can be hard to pick up; they don't have the context or the background to understand what is real. Satire requires a basic level of knowledge to be *in* on the joke. Academic research site The Conversation reported findings from communications researchers on the topic of satire. They surveyed over 800 American adults in 2019 about their beliefs in satirical articles. They divided the respondents into groups based on their political party affiliation. Members of both parties misidentified satirical articles between 6–28% of the time. The researchers found that belief in misinformation was highly influenced by the tone and political slant of the article. If the article reinforced their own political beliefs, the respondent was more likely to interpret it as true.

- **Clickbait**: Clickbait is a sensationalized headline or text/ image online that is designed to entice users to follow a link to an article on a different site. When I talk about clickbait with teens, I refer them to YouTube and half-joke, "If the YouTube video is in all caps or has three or more exclamation points, it's clickbait." Clickbait can be simply annoying or part of the next category of fake news: malicious intent.
- **Malicious intent**: When the media refers to "fake news," this is often the category we think of. Of all four, it's the rarest. The "intent" in this type of fake news is to harm another. Where this gets confusing is the word "intent." People from different faiths, political parties, beliefs, and backgrounds may assume intent from fake news, when it's simply ignorance. It's difficult to truly know the intent of the person who created the video or wrote the article. For example, an anti-vaxxer may truly believe that vaccines are harmful, so by sharing misinformation they are trying to help, but they are inadvertently harming. Their intent is positive, but the consequences are negative.
- **Propaganda**: Propaganda is information, rumors, or ideas that are deliberately spread to help or harm a person, institution, nation, or group. The intent of propaganda is not necessarily malicious, although the result of it may cause harm. The person sharing the misinformation may truly believe that their cause is the best and would benefit the world, even though their beliefs may hurt others. Propaganda is used by the right and left and has existed since early humanity. For example, the Babylonian king Hammurabi wrote many boasts about himself in his public code of laws back in 1790 BC.

When I teach fake news to teens, I speak a lot about feelings, biases, motivations, and intent. I ask the students, "What did the person mean by saying that?" This is a simple question that parents and caregivers can ask. There is not necessarily a right or wrong answer to that question, we cannot read a writer's mind. But if the answer to the question is, "I don't know," then the child hasn't thought deeply enough about the information.

After children reach upper elementary school into middle school, they are capable of this type of critical and introspective thinking. Anne Collier advocates for media literacy education. She knows that kids are looking into or encountering fringe beliefs and extreme views online:

> But to a degree we can help our kids understand that there is plenty of manipulation out there. There's clickbait, there's voyeurism, there's things that try to appeal to emotions or curiosity. Help them be alert to the manipulation and they will be able to recognize it better. All the things we talk about as adults in that regard we can talk to our kids about.

It is a delicate line to walk when educating children to distrust some information, but also trust others. You don't want to scare them or push them into nihilism. You want a healthy skepticism. They are capable of more than we think. I've had many lively discussions with tweens about fake news. Collier said, "I remember the New York State Teacher of the Year told me years ago when I interviewed him, 'there is nothing too sophisticated for a twelve-year-old mind.' Let's talk about manipulation in the media with them."

I believe in media literacy education. I've seen and studied the results. In the summer of 2019, I partnered with Professor James DiPerna who studies social emotional learning out of Penn State. We worked with two randomized classrooms of students in Grades 2–5 and tracked their change in attitudes and behaviors over the course of six weeks of digital citizenship instruction. During that time, we taught some basic media literacy concepts, and they got them.

Fourth class: Sometimes it's hard to know what's real or fake online. We can ask who, what, ___we͟r͟r͟___ and ___w͟h͟y͟___ to help figure out what's true.

Is there anything you would do to make this class better?
Circle: Yes/No
If Yes, what would you do?

How much did you enjoy today's class?

Very Sad   Sad   No Feeling   Happy   Very Happy

From pre- and post-test surveys, we found that the children were more educated about "not real" or fake things online. The children reported an attitude change that "they were more unsure about knowing if what they were finding online was real or not." I've joked to a few people that we "made children more skeptical," but that it's a success.

Even young children can start differentiating between different types of information. "I believe strongly that media literacy should be taught across disciplines in school from the earliest grades," said Dr. Kristy Roschke. "With younger students, the emphasis can be more on digital literacy and safety, but representation and persuasion can also be taught to young children in an age-appropriate fashion." Parents have a crucial role in this type of education. In the next section, I'll share additional strategies, concepts, and advice to help.

Advice for Parents and Caregivers

Media or information literacy can help children be safe online, understand better about themselves and the world around them, and be used in any classroom or career. "Media literacy should be included in all subject matters; just as other literacies are. Science, history, math—there are so many important lessons to be learned about media in these disciplines," Dr. Roschke says. But beyond the classroom, what can parents do at home? Roschke acknowledges, "it can be difficult to do . . . if parents aren't equipped to teach it." This chapter hopefully provides more tools and strategies for parents to mentor and discuss with their children the increasingly wide and varied world of information.

Know Thyself

"Know thyself" is the famous phrase attributed to ancient Greek philosophy. Legend says that the seven sages of ancient Greece gathered together at Delphi and encapsulated all their wisdom into this one command. It was believed to have been inscribed at the entrance to the Oracle of Delphi. It's a maxim that still holds true today in our technological age. By knowing yourself, your perspectives, backgrounds, thoughts, beliefs, and biases, you can better understand the effects of outside information.

Knowing yourself means knowing your "bubbles," the topics, hobbies, ideas, and framework you feel strongly about. When our bubble rubs up against a conflicting bubble, it can be an uncomfortable feeling. This uncomfortable feeling when encountering conflicting beliefs can cause someone to leave a group/platform, comment or post differing information, or even cyberbully or troll the person who supports them.

The idea of bubbles comes up in psychological research behind the topic of moral conviction. Psychology professor Dr. Linda Sitka investigates how people psychologically experience conviction versus simple preferences or conventions. These convictions are "perceived as universally and objectively true and are comparatively immune to authority or peer influence." A moral conviction would be a belief like, "abortion is always wrong," and to the person who espouses that belief it's the equivalent of 1+1=2. It's simply right; no debate. Compare this to something like a preference, "I like pepperoni pizza" or a convention, "At home we always eat dinner together on Sundays." Someone with those beliefs is more likely to budge and be open to other ideas. Convictions are like steel bubbles; they don't overlap or combine with other bubbles, they stand alone.

Much of the contention, misinformation, disinformation, and conspiracy theories can be related to these steel bubbles, or moral convictions. Dr. Sitka conducted an experiment where they brought people into an empty room with a chair that had a backpack on it. The researchers first gathered information on the strength of a person's opinion on a controversial topic. Then, they told the participant who entered the room that the person who sat there had a contrasting belief. The researcher said that the person would come back to their empty chair soon, and for the participant to pull a chair from the side of the room and take a seat. Then, they measured the distance between the "empty" chair and the participant. They found that "people with stronger moral convictions on a given issue prefer greater social and physical distance from attitudinally dissimilar users." This research has been found with children and adolescents. If a young person defines an attitude as "moral," they are less accepting of differences. Someone's strong belief "predicts greater self-reported social distance as well as prejudice, social media avoidance, anger, incivility, and antagonism toward outgroup partisans."

There is nothing inherently wrong with these strong feelings or steel bubbles. Our strong convictions create change, and often that change is for the better. We are less complacent and more active when we have a moral conviction. However, there is a negative side to these strong feelings as well. We become tribal, push others out, judge people who are different, and sometimes these feelings can turn into discrimination and violence.

Moral convictions are very difficult to change. They are part of someone's memetic framework. They help that person define who they are and how they view the world. While we may not be able to change another person's moral convictions, we can become more empathetic when we understand that there is probably someone else out there who feels as strongly as we do on a subject, but in the opposite direction. If we have this empathy, we are likely to engage differently with those people. Combatting and fighting them just reinforces their attitude that they are objectively right and everyone else is wrong. You cannot debate someone with facts when they have no doubt that they are correct. Arguing will just make them retreat further into their echo chambers and bubbles.

We might not be able to change them, but we can follow the old adage, "know thyself." Know your own bubbles. Know when you're feeling strong emotions. Know when someone else is feeling strong emotions. Know that media and online communities can reinforce someone's steel bubble. Know when to share and engage, and when to step back.

Advice for Parents of Young Children: Model

Children are not born skeptical. They believe in what they're modeled. We found this in Digital Respons-Ability's research with Grades 2–5 in 2019. At the beginning of their classes, the children did not express doubt or skepticism about media. They believed what they were told; they didn't even know they shouldn't trust it. Part of children's feelings about media comes from how they are raised.

I remember the first time my child saw an advertisement. It was around age three and we had gotten cable at home, not just streaming content. With streaming content, there were no commercials, or you could skip any advertisements. When an advertisement came on, it immediately got my preschooler's attention. First off, it was loud, and second, it was colorful and frenetic. He stared at it, confused.

If children don't have any screens, they aren't exposed to advertisements. They may assume that all content online is trustworthy. I'm not telling you to show your child ads deliberately. But think about how you were raised, with regular commercials, and how your child is currently being raised. It's probably different. So, for adults to make the assumption that children can differentiate between entertainment and persuasive advertising is a false belief. In addition, the advertising that children may be exposed to like on YouTube may be harder to decipher. Influencer advertising is subtler.

Also consider the news environment you have at home. Dr. Roschke said, "I think for parents of kids of all ages, get them engaging with news at an early age. Being aware that there is a stream of current events and it's a business . . . but that's how we find out what's happening in our world. This structure called journalism . . . is the predominant way we find information."

Perhaps when you were raised your parents watched the evening news, or listened to the news on the radio, or had a paper delivered every day. With more digital news deliberately on isolated screens, children may not be exposed to the news. Roschke reflects, "It's hard because we don't get a physical newspaper and we don't watch the news. My son doesn't often see me reading the newspaper. You have to think more intentionally." She suggests using the news to connect with what they are learning in school. Parents and caregivers can have conversations with their children about what websites to visit to find more information about that subject.

Have those conversations early. Model appropriate news use. Young children are more trusting and less skeptical of their parents. In the tween and teen years, they may not listen and talk to you as much about media. This is also the time when media can have a bigger influence. Here are some conversation-starters that parents can share with young children:

- What is your favorite show?
- What do you think will happen next in the (movie/show/game)?
- How does this (movie/show/game) make you feel?
- Do you think that's an advertisement?
- How does an advertisement make you feel? Does it want to make you get that (toy/food/game)?

Advice for Parents of Tweens: Manage
As children age, they are on the Internet more, and media has a bigger influence. "We all want to protect our kids from online harm," says Roschke, "but parents often have trouble keeping up with trends in media use, so instead they set up more draconian rules that some

kids will be tempted to break." What are your rules on media at these ages? Are your rules on media and screens inadvertently keeping your children away from news and important information?

It's a fine line to walk, encouraging safety but also curiosity. That curiosity is a normal, natural part of childhood, but that curiosity can lead children into unsafe territories. It's like taking your children to a playground. You love that they're exploring on their own—but perhaps when you see them try out the monkey bars you get a twinge in your stomach. At these older ages, parents must manage technology and let them play on their own more. "Parents can help their children be more media literate by exposing them to a wide variety of informational and entertainment media," Roschke said. "A media literate young person is one who is curious about the world and knows how to find information that can help them answer their questions." This curiosity at younger ages can lead to confidence at older ages. We want our children to develop that confidence, but that means they have to have the space to experiment, play, try and sometimes fail.

We also need to "know thyself" just like our children. Are our emotional reactions and fears driving our rules and decision-making? Is the threat really as large or scary as we think it is? When we react so emotionally with our children, we lose our credibility. At young ages, people who have authority and credibility with children are a small group: parents, teachers, babysitters, family, church leaders. But as children become tweens, that circle of credibility and authority widens. Children may follow an influencer, streamer, celebrity, sports star, or others. And that small group of earlier authorities has to compete for attention. Parents who automatically dismiss the online influences of their children as trivial or dumb can lose some of that credibility. Parents should explain to their tween in more detail why an influencer should or shouldn't have someone's trust or attention. Trust is earned and parents shouldn't assume that they will always be the most credible source in someone's life.

This trust should not only be built with parents but also with other institutions, processes, methods, and theories. Roschke talks about seeing this in her undergraduate journalism classes:

> I think this happens at all ages. I see this with the undergrads I teach in college. We don't really explain what the credible sources are and why. We give them textbooks and I'm sure they surmise if it's important enough to be in the textbook it's credible, but we never talk about why these people are cited in the textbook. We don't teach why we teach the scientific method. We don't talk about how we came to know the issues we know. Why would I trust the CDC? Why would I trust the Supreme Court? Why would I trust QAnon? We don't talk about that. When we do credit or discredit it is very much opinion based or emotionally driven. Then at a certain point when our kids stop trusting us that might be part of the reason why.

Here are some conversation starters for tweens as they independently explore media:

- What is that advertisement trying to say?
- Do you know why we have these media rules in the home?
- Do you know why I believe in that (news story/organization, etc.)?
- Do you think that's an accurate website? Why or why not?
- Why do you think they shared that post?

Advice for Parents of Teens: Monitor

As children age, their trust in parents and the larger world declines and their skepticism rises. This is hard to watch, but normal. Teens are growing and preparing for independence. They are discovering and establishing their own identities. Despite this growth, teens are vulnerable to misinformation and conspiracy theories. While the emotional centers in their brains are fully developed, their prefrontal cortex is still changing. They feel emotions strongly. Their brains are gas pedals without brakes.

Misinformation spreads faster and wider when we are emotionally driven. A study published in *Science* examined how false news spread from data from Twitter for over a decade. The researchers found that "falsehood diffused significantly farther, faster, deeper, and more broadly than the truth in all categories of information . . . false news inspired fear, disgust, and surprise in replies." Teenagers, who experience strong emotions because of puberty, changing hormones, and this busy stage of life may be more susceptible to believing and sharing misinformation.

Teens don't consume news the same way as adults. "Most people don't have a regular news habit, which is part of the reason we are where we are," Roschke said. Teens may only be exposed to the news from vents from friends, clickbait on news feeds, or headlines. They get small bits of information that lack nuance and depth but are packed with feeling.

Adolescents, unlike younger children, are more aware of persuasive communication and advertisements. "They are very aware that they are being sold something all the time. All the influencers that they follow and the ways in which people are selling something. It makes them very cynical," said Roschke. She worries about this cynicism because "it doesn't make them healthily skeptical. But then if they see something they think is real they don't question it." The high degree of peer influence on tweens and teens can lead a young person to believe misinformation if it's shared from a friend. Alternatively, adolescents distrust parents and other authority figures more, so information shared from those sources may be even less trusted.

How can parents, who grew up in an age of more information scarcity, help adolescents who live in a world of information abundance?

- **Discuss deeper**. Discuss the whys of behavior, motivations, biases, cultural and societal norms, and more. Talk about the role of money and advertising in media. Teens are fully capable of understanding deeper concepts.

- **Give alternatives**. Don't punish around media; they may just find a way around you to access it. Provide alternatives instead. If you're concerned about a certain site they are on, show them alternative sites.
- **Have a digital media diary**. If media use is a concern, have your child track their usage for a week. This is an activity that Dr. Roschke does with her students. The students track what sites and how long they are on them and then self-reflect on their usage. Parents should also join in on creating their own media diary.

Parents should monitor, not mandate media use. Your child needs space for exploration to learn about the world around them. Soon they will be independent and away from you in that world. Here are some conversation starters for teens as they consume media:

- What do you think that (show/movie/meme, etc.) is trying to say? Why do you think it's saying that?
- Who funds that (website/show/account)?
- What platforms do you use to get the news? Do you think there are other ones out there that you would like?
- How do you feel when you read the news?
- Let's talk about (name current event). What do you think?

Media literacy continues to be my biggest concern online. With the current misinformation landscape, it's become even more important to me. Sometimes I get overwhelmed and burdened, too. I wonder, what kind of world is my child growing up in? Can I help them as they navigate this? Will my child fall into one of these online echo chambers? But I recognize that even without the Internet, there have always been polarizing feelings, in and out groups, tribalism, bias, and more. The Internet exacerbated and accentuated these issues but did not create them. Regarding these media issues, Dr. Kristy Roschke says, "these are not technology problems but society problems." Media is a reflection of society's norms and values. While we may not be able to control everything in the media, we can work to create our own norms and values in our families. We can create our own healthy bubbles.

Chapter 9
Online Opportunities

THIS past year my young son had a business idea. He wanted to create a "sweets" business, modeled on his favorite stuffed hedgehog. I admit, my first reaction was a question of exactly *who* would be making these treats; I reminded him that his mother had little to no cooking skills. But then I stepped back and realized that this could be a fun learning opportunity, a chance to teach him some basic business principles, and to use technology in a positive way. I then asked him to develop a logo and explained that a logo was a word and/or image used to represent something. He thought hard on what he wanted in a logo and came up with this illustration:

I took the illustration and logged on to Fiverr, a platform for freelancers to connect with buyers around the world. We looked at several freelancer's portfolios, noting their costs, and what images aligned with his vision of Hedgie's Sweets. After some time and conversation, he picked out a freelancer and we submitted a work order together. After that, there was some back and forth, refining the logo. He would ask me "did they message you yet?" eagerly awaiting the next draft. Finally, we had a finished product:

I remember when I was around his age, I had my own little business selling my old toys to kids in the neighborhood. I would put out a table in my driveway in the hot summer sun and walk up and down the street trying to find customers. My reach for my toy reselling business was as far as I could get on my scooter. Now, if I wanted to run that toy reselling business, I'd have a wealth of platforms and communication tools at my disposal. Like Hedgie's Sweets, I could easily create a logo or get other graphics made. I could sell the toys to an international market on eBay or reach kids in other neighborhoods by posting on social media. If a kid came to my table, as they sometimes did, with the wrong change or no cash, I could take payments in other ways. In Hedgie's Sweet's official debut at a joint yard sale, he sold his cookies through Venmo as well as cash. Information about his business was shared on the neighborhood Facebook page, reaching more people. Technology provides an amazing opportunity for young people that parents did not have when they were young. What are those opportunities? And what can parents do to help their children thrive in a twenty-first-century online world?

The Digital Economy

Young people are participating more and more in the digital economy. When you hear the word "economy" you may immediately think of buying and selling online. That's part of it, but the digital economy encompasses a wider range of activities: collaboration, reputation building and management, interactive gaming, creating content, advocacy, and more. Alexa Hasse is a research associate with the Berkman Klein Center for Internet & Society at Harvard University. She was part of a June 2020 report by the university called "Youth and the Digital Economy: Exploring Youth Practices, Motivations, Skills, Pathways, and Value Creation." The report says, "The Internet and digital technologies that run on top of it have unleashed an explosion of creative opportunities for youth to be active in 'participatory' and 'networked' cultures." The report notes the entrepreneurial opportunities, like with Hedgie's Sweets, writing "another important consequence of an emerging digital economy is the profound effect it has had on youth and their ability to be more entrepreneurial." Alexa Hasse sees these opportunities, saying, "Through digital technologies, young people are encountering opportunities to act as consumers, producers, and users."

Everyone online is a user or a consumer of content. If you've watched a YouTube video or scrolled a newsfeed, you're a consumer or user. It's easy to consume, harder to produce. Hasse notes that what a lot of us do online is both consume and produce; we're "prosumers." "The term 'prosumer' combines the word 'producer' with 'consumer' to describe this new duality," she said. "These production practices may range from posting a photo on Instagram or commenting on a friend's status update on Facebook to the more active end of the spectrum—creating a YouTube tutorial, or developing content using programming." Prosuming requires more participation, engagement, and digital literacies than simply consuming. Being able to produce content can provide those entrepreneurial opportunities, as well as making one an active, rather than passive, participant in the world.

How do we define online consumption? It depends on the person and their age. "When we look at media creation, some literature indicates that youth do not report high levels of media production," says Hasse:

> Others, however, note that selecting, commenting on, and sharing information with friends *is* a participatory act. And currently, when young people take part in media creation, it's often less likely to take previous forms that were more common (i.e., amateur filmmakers developing videos). It's typically instead expressed through new means, like sending a GIF over a text message, or sharing a video with friends on Snapchat.

Parents and educators may have a different understanding of what is "worthwhile" and "engaging" online. I've heard from teens that their parents dismiss their technology use as trivial or frivolous. The teens see what they are doing as active and important, but the adults just see a "silly" video or meme. For adults to help their children create digital opportunities and navigate the online economy, they will need to reexamine their own biases and be more open-minded. Alexa Hasse says:

> It's then crucial to value the entire spectrum of participation and the extent to which even modest participation can lead to opportunities for identity exploration, learning, and cultivating a sense of belonging or community. Additionally, what may seem as mundane participation in isolation, such as the sharing of a video on TikTok or a comment on Instagram, can potentially, over time, have a societal effect (e.g., toward

movements advocating for racial justice, or gender equality). If we take all these points together, it's important to note that we have to move away from an adult-normative view of what online participation should look like and consider participation from a more nuanced lens.

What does healthy production and prosuming look like? Like Hasse said, envision online participation as a spectrum, not as a black-and-white list of dos and donts.

Consumers to Creators in the Digital World:

Where are you?

Consumers of content	Prosumers Producing and consuming content	Creators Creating content
Watching YouTube	Liking a post	Writing and sharing a post
Watching television	Reading and commenting on an online article	Playing a game with friends or family
Scrolling a feed	Anonymously posting on a message board	Writing an article
		Posting a picture you took on Instagram
Playing a game by yourself	Commenting on a YouTube video	Sharing art you made on a message board
Reading an online article	Commenting on a live stream	Creating your own video for YouTube

Another way is through online collaboration. Adults do this all the time in the workplace, especially with remote work. Collaborating online is an important life and work skill. Hasse shares an example from her report, "Youth in the Digital Economy":

For instance, in our report on youth and the digital economy, we highlight a case study of virtual collaboration on Scratch. For context, Scratch is an online programming language and learning community based at the MIT media lab where young people ages 8–15 from around the world can work together to build animations, games, and other creative content. We took a case study of youth who created a multiple animator project, or MAP, on Scratch called "Hands for Orlando," which was a tribute to the victims of the Pulse nightclub shooting in Orlando in 2016. A MAP is a self-organized small group, ranging from 12 to 40 participants, that works together to produce an animated music video.

The young people worked together with adults and stakeholders to create this video tribute that was shared on social media. Through this online collaboration, the young people learned to better create tasks and stay on them, define objectives and goals, communicate with others, and hone their technical skills. Hasse describes all the different skills needed for this project, and other work online. "A range of competencies are needed to successfully participate in our rapidly evolving digital economy, from technical skills (e.g., knowing how to use digital technologies to achieve a certain goal, like finding specific information online), to social and emotional skills (e.g., empathy, collaboration)." An online collaborative project can teach a wealth of information. And there are many such projects online. Wikipedia is an example of a long-running collaborative project, but young people can be involved in work across fields of advocacy, creative fields, science, psychology, and more. The next section will describe how these online opportunities can positively impact young people's college experience and careers.

College and Career

Children grow up quickly and it seems one day you're concerned with diapers, the next, diplomas. The Internet is an amazing tool to help parents prepare their children for college and their careers (and, yes, it helps with diapers, too). In the teen years, parents need to shift their mindset from managing children's Internet use to monitoring.

This means stepping back; not intervening unless necessary and looking at the online world not as a place rife with dangers, but with opportunities.

Basic digital literacy skills are essential for any job. These are skills easier to teach, and your child will almost certainly get the basics in school. But employers want more than the basics, they want employees who are adaptable, flexible, and have the soft skills to back up the hard skills.

In early 2020, LinkedIn reported on the most important job skills based on data from their network of 660 million users and 20 million job postings. They divided these skills into hard skills and soft skills. Parents are essential for teaching soft skills because they aren't easily taught in a classroom. These are interpersonal skills that are difficult to measure. Hard and soft skills can be nurtured online, but only by children who are given the opportunity.

The soft skills LinkedIn listed for 2020 are, in order:

1. Creativity
2. Persuasion
3. Collaboration
4. Adaptability
5. Emotional intelligence

Most of these soft skills were the same as in 2019. Since then, an increase in remote learning due to COVID-19 has highlighted the importance of these soft skills even more, as students, teachers, parents, and employees were required to quickly adapt, and online collaboration was needed to quickly pivot. The pandemic also forced people to take learning into their own hands. Without in-person managers or teachers, people had to find the information on their own. At an October 2020 LinkedIn learning summit, there were conversations about how important learning was in 2020 and beyond. The VP of Learning & Development at LinkedIn, Kevin Delaney, said of learning, "it's no longer a nice-to-have. It's a must-have and essential to success." A fall 2020 LinkedIn learning survey of professionals reported that COVID-19 made a culture of learning even more vital.

Teaching is easier than ever before. Parents and caregivers may remember the days when they had to search through stacks of books and dig through newspapers and magazines hoping to find the information they needed. Today, that information is near instant and easy to access. We all, young people especially, have the opportunity to take charge of our own learning at our own pace. But that learning does require soft skills, like those in the LinkedIn list, and the ability to critically evaluate information. Alexa Hasse encourages parents:

> Expand your definition of "education." When many of us think of education, our mind immediately shifts to a classroom. But there is an array of rich educational opportunities outside of the formal learning environment—in libraries, museums, volunteer organizations, and online. For example, YouTube is not only for entertainment purposes—it also offers many channels that are educational. And platforms such as Khan Academy help young people learn math outside of school.

COVID-19 has dramatically shifted how we work and learn online. Hasse acknowledges this and states, "In the context of COVID, as so much is now moving online, skills like online collaboration and communication will become all the more essential for youth to participate and thrive in society and economy."

It can be difficult for parents to see the skill-building and education in their child's typical Internet use. An adult who just sees their teen talking to friends all the time may not see persuasion in their communication, or creativity through making or sharing memes or Snaps. They may perceive that their child has too much screen time on YouTube, when actually their kid is learning new and valuable information. Parents should monitor their child's screen time but do so nonjudgmentally and with an open mind. Who knows, maybe you'll learn something new from your child!

Some open-minded questions parents can ask their older children and teens about their tech use include:

- What is your favorite app?
- What do you do on that app?
- What's a subject that you're really curious about now?
- What's your favorite YouTube channel?
- Who do you want to be online?

In 2017–2018, we at Digital Respons-Ability surveyed secondary students about their interests in STEM (Science, Technology, Engineering, and Math) and technology. We asked them before and after the classes to respond with how they felt about statements like, "I do science and technology activities that are not for school," and "I would like to have a job related to technology." Through these pre- and post-test surveys, we found a correlation between students' interest in and knowledge of digital citizenship, and their interest in STEM and technology. Students who reported that they "like" digital citizenship or that they knew more of those principles also said that they were more interested in STEM and technology. This correlation stayed the same with different ages and populations. This correlation makes intuitive sense. Students who feel more confident online, who see themselves as empowered and knowledgeable enough to navigate technology, would be more comfortable with those types of careers.

Digital Access

This book has operated with the assumption that your family has digital access. If you've picked up a book on digital parenting, technology is most likely a big part of your life. But that assumption does not hold true with many families in the United States, and around the world. I saw this anecdotally in my role as a librarian in a low-income area. Children would come to the library every day after school to access the Internet and do their homework on public computers. They would sometimes stay until we closed at 9:00 p.m. Outside of school, the library was the only place these students could go to reliably access the Internet and computers.

While we don't have exact numbers, the Federal Communications Commission (FCC) estimates that at least 21 million Americans lack broadband access. But the definition of broadband access can be unclear. For example, if someone has slow Internet, where they can't stream or they have difficulty watching videos, is that truly equitable access? With remote learning, multiple family members are often using the Internet at home, and slow speeds can be extremely limiting. A 2019 Microsoft report on rural Americans upped the FCC's estimate; they found that around 162 million Americans did not have high-speed Internet access.

The COVID-19 pandemic has heightened these inequalities. Surveys near the beginning of the COVID-19 pandemic by Pew Research found that a fifth of parents said it was likely their children would not be able to finish their homework because they didn't have a computer and/or Wi-Fi. A report from UCLA researchers echoed this gap in digital access found by Pew. They analyzed census data between April and July of 2020 and found that while computer and Internet service for children's education was more widespread, this access was not distributed equally. Low-income households and Hispanic and black families had less digital access than other groups. A summary of the report said, "Unchecked, the digital inequality threatens to widen the racial and income gap in educational achievement and contributes to a reproduction of intergenerational inequality."

This gap in digital access, called the homework gap, means that children, through no fault of their own, may fall behind in school just because they don't have the hardware and/or high-speed Internet at home. Over time, the absences, falling grades, and incomplete assignments can create division between the haves and have-nots that can persist past school. While there are some legitimate dangers and concerns about online access, perhaps a bigger danger is no access at all.

Digital access is an issue worldwide, not just in the United States. Amitabh Kumar, founder of Social Media Matters, is a digital parenting instructor who has coordinated over 1,000 workshops for parents across India. He said, "The digital divide is ever-increasing, and the ones not connected via a smartphone are totally left behind. We in India live in different centuries at the same time. I think we need to invest heavily in infrastructure to ensure we work on development of all and not just a selected privileged few."

Kumar works with parents who are afraid of technology, and parents who wish they had technology. He describes the group of parents who have access as three categories: "Parents who let their kids be unattended on the Internet. Parents who explore the web together with their children (though a minority in numbers), and finally the majority who are super scared of all things related to the Internet. Their fears revolve around pornography and their kids interacting with strangers."

The fears of parents without digital access are different. Kumar said that "70 percent of India still has to get connected to broadband Internet. In order to have a positive online educational experience, we need to give this 70 percent a fair playing field." The majority of Indian families during the COVID-19 pandemic were negatively affected. With no Internet access, children were cut off from school, parents from employment and other services, and families were isolated during lockdown. "Children belonging to economically weaker sections are unable to keep up with rich kids," Kumar said. "This leads to helpless parents and children dropping out of school." While families with high-speed broadband access in India were fearful of pornography and online strangers, families without access were worried about their children's long-term educational prospects.

There is a digital divide between online access, and a divide between parents' perceptions of technology. My experience echoes what Kumar has found. I taught a series of classes to refugee parents, who typically live in low-income areas. At those classes, the parents were mainly concerned with how to use mobile devices, settings, the software, and apps out there. Generally, they wanted their children to be online. They saw their mobile phone as a connection to their home country, family overseas, and job opportunities. Contrast this with classes I've done in higher-income areas. The concerns there are more around online safety and screen time. In my teaching many parents and talking to others like Amitbah Kumar, I've come to realize that fears around pornography, instead of fears around failing school, are a luxury that not everyone is lucky enough to have.

This is not to dismiss people's fears—but to put them in perspective. When you step back and think about it, aren't we amazingly fortunate to be worried about online activity rather than having enough food to eat? We live in an amazing, and stressful, time with so much information, entertainment, and opportunity. Young people have more access and freedoms online than any previous generation. Parents can help their children responsibly access those opportunities. "As our society and economy become increasingly digitally connected, I think that young peoples' role in the digital economy will only become more prominent over time—if we also address disparities in access and skills in the context of digital technologies," Alexa Hasse said.

Parents should keep in mind the 3 Ms of Digital Parenting framework. Starting from a young age, parents can model healthy online behavior, then step back to manage their children's access, and finally monitor their children's online creations and participation in the digital economy. These gradual steps as children age can better set up a child for their own independent digital identities and online futures. Yes, there are fears. I'm a parent myself and have my own worries about my child and the larger online world. But fears can hold us and our children back. Despite our own feelings, we must be fearless digital parents.

Appendix

Technology Conversation Starters for Parents

Model: Ages 0–8
- Show me how you do that on (name of the device).
- What is your favorite thing to do on (name of the device)?
- Why is that your favorite thing to do?
- What do you think will happen next in the (movie/show/game)?
- When I'm on my phone, how does it make you feel?
- Can I have permission to share this (picture/video/quote) of yours?
- How does that (movie/show/game) make you feel?

Manage: Ages 8–13
- What things are private to you? What things are public?
- How would you feel if someone shared something private about you online without your permission? Can I do better about asking your permission?
- Will you be able to finish your homework on time to (play/watch etc.)?
- Who are your friends online?
- What do your friends like to do online?
- Do those friends ever do things that make you (uncomfortable/mad/sad)? What do you do when you feel uncomfortable?

- What are some things you like to do online with me and the rest of your family? What is something we do that you don't like?
- How do you feel about how much time I spend online? How can I improve?

Monitor: Ages 13–18

- What do you think that (show/movie/GIF/meme, etc.) is trying to say? Why do you think it's saying that?
- How does social media make you feel? If it makes you feel (uncomfortable/mad/sad) what's something you can do to feel better?
- What would you tell a friend who shared something online that probably should have been kept private?
- If a friend told you that you shared something private, or that made them feel uncomfortable, how would you feel? What would you do?
- How does technology affect dating relationships? What do you see?
- What's something positive you can do online today?
- How do you want others to view you online?

Questions to Ask When Creating a Family Media Plan/Digital Contract

- What are tech-free times?
- Who is responsible for charging/repairing the device?
- Will this device be shared with friends or other family members?
- What information must be shared with parents?
- What information should I *not* share with others?
- What happens if the device is lost?
- What are the passwords to the device?
- Who purchases apps/games and other things for the device?
- If the rules aren't followed in this contract, what should happen?

Digital Contract Template

I _____, agree to:

Tech-free times
(Fill in details: times on and off, limits, etc.)

Responsibilities for the device
(Fill in details: charging, repairing, etc.)

Sharing
(Fill in details: information parents should know, who gets to use the device, what not to share, etc.)

Passwords
(Fill in passwords)

Consequences
(Fill in passwords)
This family media plan is active when everyone signs it. We will revisit the plan on _____.

_____

Child's signature and date

_____

Parent's signature and date

For more information on Family Media Plans, check out HealthyChildren *.org with the American Academy of Pediatrics.*

References

Chapter 1

Doom (1993 video game). (2020, April 26). Retrieved April 26, 2020, from https://en.wikipedia.org/wiki/Doom_(1993_video_game).

Irvine, R., & Kincaid, C. (1999, May 10). Video Games Can Kill. Retrieved April 26, 2020, from https://web.archive.org/web/20071005011325/http://www.aim.org/media_monitor/A3327_0_2_0_C/.

Miller, G. E. (2020, January 13). The U.S. is the Most Overworked Nation in the World. Retrieved December 26, 2020, from https://20something finance.com/american-hours-worked-productivity-vacation/.

Owenby, T. (2020, August 25). What can the US learn from South Korea's testing pressures? Retrieved April 26, 2020, from https://theconversation .com/what-can-the-us-learn-from-south-koreas-testing-pressures -40365.

Rogers-Whitehead, C. (2018, October 11). If your kids are using anonymous messaging app Lipsi, they probably shouldn't. Retrieved April 26, 2020, from https://www.ksl.com/article/46404784/if-your-kids -are-using-anonymous-messaging-app-lipsi-they-probably-shouldnt.

Chapter 2

About ASQ. (2018, October 25). Retrieved July 19, 2020, from https://agesandstages.com/about-asq/.

Bandura, Albert. "Self-efficacy Mechanism in Human Agency," *American Psychologist* 37. No. 2 (1982).122–147. doi:10.1037/0003-066X.37.2.122.

Brain Architecture. (2019, August 20). Retrieved July 19, 2020, from https://developingchild.harvard.edu/science/key-concepts/brain -architecture/.

Carr, Peggy G. (2017, May 24). "A First Look at the 2015 Program for International Student Assessment Financial Literacy," *Institute of Education Sciences, National Center for Education Statistics.*

Carrns, A. (2020, February 07). More States Require Students to Learn About Money Matters. Retrieved July 24, 2020, from https://www .nytimes.com/2020/02/07/your-money/states-financial-education .html.

Clay, Rebecca A. (March 2016). "Albert Bandura receives National Medal of Science". *Monitor on Psychology.* 47 (3): 8.

Galinsky, E. (2010). *Mind in the Making: The seven essential life skills every child needs.* New York, NY: William Marrow.

Gennaro, L. (2020, December 04). 68 Useful eCommerce Statistics You Must Know in 2020. Retrieved December 26, 2020, from https: //wpforms.com/ecommerce-statistics/.

Lombana-Bermudez, Andres, Sandra Cortesi, et. al. (2020) "Youth and the Digital Economy: Exploring Youth Practices, Motivations, Skills, Pathways, and Value Creation," Youth and Media, Berkman Klein Center for Internet & Society. Retrieved from https://cyber.harvard. edu/publication/2020/youth-and-digital-economy.

Madigan S, Browne D, Racine N, Mori C, Tough S. Association Between Screen Time and Children's Performance on a Developmental Screening Test. *JAMA Pediatr.* 2019;173(3):244–250. doi:10.1001 /jamapediatrics.2018.5056.

N., P. (2015, July 10). Developmental Stage. Retrieved July 19, 2020, from https://psychologydictionary.org/developmental-stage.

Spagnola, M., & Fiese, B. H. (2007). Family Routines and Rituals. *Infants & Young Children, 20*(4), 284–299. doi:10.1097/01.iyc.0000290352 .32170.5a.

Vandenberg, B. (n.d.). Magical Thinking. Retrieved July 24, 2020, from https://www.britannica.com/science/magical-thinking.

Chapter 3

APA. (2020, May 21). High stress related to coronavirus is the new normal for many parents, says new APA survey. Retrieved October 5, 2020, from https://www.sciencedaily.com/releases/2020/05/200521151919.htm.

Cheng, E., & Wilkinson, T. (2020, April 13). Agonizing Over Screen Time? Follow the Three C's. Retrieved October 2, 2020, from https:

//www.nytimes.com/2020/04/13/parenting/manage-screen-time
-coronavirus.html.

Christakis, E. (2018, June 16). The Dangers of Distracted Parenting. Retrieved
October 5, 2020, from https://www.theatlantic.com/magazine/archive
/2018/07/the-dangers-of-distracted-parenting/561752/.

Colorado Libraries for Early Literacy (n.d.). Five Early Literacy
Practices. Retrieved September 23, 2020, from https://www.clel.org
/fiveearlyliteracypractices.

Every Child Ready to Read. (n.d.). Retrieved September 23, 2020, from
http://everychildreadytoread.org/.

Healthy Digital Media Use Habits for Babies, Toddlers & Preschoolers.
(n.d.). Retrieved October 2, 2020, from https://www.healthychildren.
org/English/family-life/Media/Pages/Healthy-Digital-Media-Use
-Habits-for-Babies-Toddlers-Preschoolers.aspx.

Johnson, David Jackson, "Parents' Perceptions of Smartphone Use and
Parenting Practices" (2017). UNLV Theses, Dissertations, Professional
Papers, and Capstones. 3141. Retrieved October 2, 2020, from https:
//digitalscholarship.unlv.edu/thesesdissertations/3141.

Lindsey, Eric W. "Preschool children's friendships and peer acceptance:
Links to social competence." Child Study Journal 32, no. 3 (2002):
145-156.

Nestmann, F., & Hurrelmann, K. (1994). Social networks and social support
in childhood and adolescence (pp. 20–21). Berlin: Walter de Gruyter.

Pappas, S. (2020, April 1). What do we really know about kids and screens?
Retrieved September 23, 2020, from https://www.apa.org/monitor
/2020/04/cover-kids-screens.

Rideout, V., & Robb, M. B. (2020). The Common Sense census: Media
use by kids age zero to eight, 2020. San Francisco, CA: Common
Sense Media.

Spagnola, M., & Fiese, B. H. (2007). Family Routines and Rituals. Infants
& Young Children, 20(4), 284–299. doi:10.1097/01.iyc.0000290352
.32170.5a.

Weir, K. (2014, June). The lasting impact of neglect. Retrieved October 5,
2020, from https://www.apa.org/monitor/2014/06/neglect.

Chapter 4

Booker, C. L., Kelly, Y. J. & Sacker, A. Gender differences in the associations between age trends of social media interaction and well-being

among 10-15 year olds in the UK. BMC Public Health 18, 321 (2018). https://doi.org/10.1186/s12889-018-5220-4.

Media Use by Tweens and Teens 2019: Infographic: Common Sense Media. (2019, October 28). Retrieved March 17, 2020, from https://www .commonsensemedia.org/Media-use-by-tweens-and-teens-2019 -infographic.

Parenthood, P. (n.d.). Goals of Sex Education for Teenagers: Youth Health Services. Retrieved March 17, 2020, from https://www.planned parenthood.org/learn/for-educators/what-are-goals-sex-education -youth.

Rogers-Whitehead, Carrie. "Rise of the Dumb Phones: 5 Alternatives to Smartphones," KSL.com, August 21, 2018. https://www.ksl.com /article/46379304/rise-of-the-dumb-phones-5-alternatives-to-smart phones.

Shipman, C. (2018, September 21). How Puberty Kills Girls' Confidence. Retrieved October 5, 2020, from https://www.theatlantic.com/family /archive/2018/09/puberty-girls-confidence/563804/.

Steinberg, L., & Monahan, K. C. (2007). Age differences in resistance to peer influence. *Developmental psychology*, 43(6), 1531–1543.

Trekels, Jolien, and Steven Eggermont. 2018. "'I Can/Should Look Like a Media Figure': The Association Between Direct and Indirect Media Exposure and Teens' Sexualizing Appearance Behaviors." *Journal of Sex Research* 55 (3): 320–33. doi:10.1080/00224499.2017.1387754.

Chapter 5

Casey, B. J. (2015). Beyond Simple Models of Self-Control to Circuit-Based Accounts of Adolescent Behavior. *Annual Review of Psychology*, 66(1), 295–319. doi:10.1146/annurev-psych-010814-015156.

Connected Learning Alliance (2020, August 04). Teens' Social Media Use Isn't the Problem. Retrieved August 20, 2020, from https: //clalliance.org/blog/teens-social-media-use-isnt-the-problem/?utm _source=mailchimp.com.

Coyne, Sarah M., Adam A. Rogers, Jessica D. Zurcher, Laura Stockdale, and Mccall Booth. "Does Time Spent Using Social Media Impact Mental Health?: An Eight Year Longitudinal Study." *Computers in Human Behavior* 104 (2020): 106160. https://doi.org/10.1016/j .chb.2019.106160.

Ghekiere, A., Van Cauwenberg, J., Vandendriessche, A. et al. Trends in sleeping difficulties among European adolescents: Are these associated with physical inactivity and excessive screen time?. *Int J Public Health* 64, 487–498 (2019). https://doi.org/10.1007/s00038-018-1188-1.

Lombana-Bermudez, Andres, Sandra Cortesi, et. al. (2020) "Youth and the Digital Economy: Exploring Youth Practices, Motivations, Skills, Pathways, and Value Creation," Youth and Media, Berkman Klein Center for Internet & Society. Retrieved from https://cyber.harvard.edu/publication/2020/youth-and-digital-economy.

Love is Respect.org. "Help my Child," Retrieved August 20, 2020, from https://www.loveisrespect.org/for-someone-else/help-my-child/.

Love is Respect.org. "Love is Digital," Retrieved August 20, 2020, from https://www.loveisrespect.org/for-someone-else/help-my-child/.

Morin, Amy. "The Developmental Milestones 18-Year-Olds Reach." Verywell Family, July 15, 2019. https://www.verywellfamily.com/18-year-old-developmental-milestones-2609030.

National Research Council (US) and Institute of Medicine (US) Forum on Adolescence; Kipke MD, editor. Adolescent Development and the Biology of Puberty: Summary of a Workshop on New Research. Washington (DC): National Academies Press (US); 1999. Adolescent Development and the Biology of Puberty. Retrieved from: https://www.ncbi.nlm.nih.gov/books/NBK224692/.

Neighmond, P. (2018, December 12). Sleepless No More In Seattle - Later School Start Time Pays Off For Teens. Retrieved August 20, 2020, from https://www.npr.org/sections/health-shots/2018/12/12/676118782/sleepless-no-more-in-seattle-later-school-start-time-pays-off-for-teens.

Parenthood, P. (n.d.). Healthy Relationships For Teens: Tips & Advice to Help You. Retrieved August 20, 2020, from https://www.plannedparenthood.org/learn/teens/relationships/relationships-101/having-healthy-relationship.

"Sleep for Teenagers." Sleep Foundation, June 1, 2020. https://www.sleepfoundation.org/articles/teens-and-sleep.

Walker, Matthew. *Why We Sleep: the New Science of Sleep and Dreams*. London: Allan Lane an imprint of Penguin Books, 2018.

Zephoria, "The Top 10 Valuable Snapchat Statistics." (2020, November 03). Retrieved August 20, 2020, from https://zephoria.com/top-10-valuable-snapchat-statistics/.

Chapter 6

Allyn, B. (2020, August 04). Class-Action Lawsuit Claims TikTok Steals Kids' Data And Sends It To China. Retrieved August 9, 2020, from https://www.npr.org/2020/08/04/898836158/class-action-lawsuit-claims-tiktok-steals-kids-data-and-sends-it-to-china.

Baca, M. (2019, November 07). Internet freedom declines in U.S. for third consecutive year. Retrieved August 3, 2020, from https://www.washingtonpost.com/technology/2019/11/07/Internet-freedom-declines-us-third-consecutive-year/.

Brown, Jane D. and Kelly L. L'Engle. 2009. " X-Rated: Sexual Attitudes and Behaviors Associated With U.S. Early Adolescents' Exposure to Sexually Explicit Media." *Communication Research* 36 : 1 : 129 – 151. https://doi.org/10.1177/0093650208326465.

CNN. (2020, July 01). White supremacists openly organize racist violence on Telegram, report finds. Retrieved August 9, 2020, from https://www.channel3000.com/white-supremacists-openly-organize-racist-violence-on-telegram-report-finds/.

Cyberbullying Research Center C. (2020, December 01). "Cyberbullying Facts." Retrieved August 3, 2020, from https://cyberbullying.org/facts.

David-Ferdon, C., Vivolo-Kantor, A. M., Dahlberg, L. L., Marshall, K. J., Rainford, N. & Hall, J. E. (2016). A Comprehensive Technical Package for the Prevention of Youth Violence and Associated Risk Behaviors. Atlanta, GA: National Center for Injury Prevention and Control, Centers for Disease Control and Prevention. https://www.cdc.gov/violenceprevention/pdf/yv-technicalpackage.pdf.

Emmers-Sommer, Tara M. 2018. "Reasons for Pornography Consumption: Associations with Gender, Psychological and Physical Sexual Satisfaction, and Attitudinal Impacts." *Sexuality & Culture* 22 (1): 48–62. doi:10.1007/s12119-017-9452-8.

Halliday, J. (2019, December 30). Thousands of children under 14 have been investigated by police for sexting. Retrieved August 9, 2020, from https://www.theguardian.com/society/2019/dec/30/thousands-of-children-under-14-have-been-investigated-by-police-for-sexting.

Harvey, Carissa A., Tiffany A. Harvey, and Ashley E. Thompson. 2020. "The 'Sextual' Double Standard: An Experimental Examination of Variations in Judgments of Men and Women Who Engage in

Computer-Mediated Sexual Communication." *Sexuality & Culture* 24 (3): 712–32. doi:10.1007/s12119-019-09658-8.

Hinduja, Sameer. "It Is Time to Teach Safe Sexting." Cyberbullying Research Center, January 16, 2020. https://cyberbullying.org/it-is-time -to-teach-safe-sexting.

Key Internet Statistics to Know in 2020 (Including Mobile). (n.d.). Retrieved August 7, 2020, from https://www.broadbandsearch.net /blog/Internet-statistics.

Kowalski, R. W., & Limber, S. (2013, July 1). Psychological, Physical, and Academic Correlates of Cyberbullying and Traditional Bullying. Retrieved August 3, 2020, from https://doi.org/10.1016/j.jadohealth .2012.09.018.

Livingstone, S. Stoilova, M. and Nandagiri, R. (2018) Children's data and privacy online: Growing up in a digital age. An evidence Review. London: London School of Economics and Political Science.

Mozur, P. (2019, April 14). One Month, 500,000 Face Scans: How China Is Using A.I. to Profile a Minority. Retrieved October 26, 2020, from https://www.nytimes.com/2019/04/14/technology/china-surveillance -artificial-intelligence-racial-profiling.html.

National Center for Missing and Exploited Children, "Child Sex Trafficking in America," Retrieved August 9, 2020, from https://www .missingkids.org/content/dam/missingkids/pdfs/CSTinAmerica _ParentsGuardians.pdf.

Patchin, J. (2019, July 10). "Summary of Our Cyberbullying Research (2004–2016)." Retrieved August 7, 2020, from https://cyberbullying .org/summary-of-our-cyberbullying-research.

Peter, J. & Valkenburg, P.M. (2016). Adolescents and Pornography: A Review of 20 Years of Research. *The Journal of Sex Research* 53(4–5), 209–531. https://www.nytimes.com/2018/02/07/magazine/teenagers -learning-online-porn-literacy-sex-education.html Accessed September 6, 2020.

Reuters Staff. (2020, July 31). Facebook raises settlement to $650 million in facial recognition lawsuit. Retrieved August 26, 2020, from https: //www.reuters.com/article/us-facebook-privacy-lawsuit/facebook- raises-settlement-to-650-million-in-facial-recognition-lawsuit- idUSKCN24W313.

Ringrose J, Harvey L, Gill R, Livingstone S. Teen girls, sexual double standards and 'sexting': Gendered value in digital image exchange. *Feminist Theory*. 2013; 14: 305–323. 10.1177/1464700113499853.

Rothman, Emily F. Daley, Nicole and Alder, Jess, "A Pornography Literacy Program for Adolescents", *American Journal of Public Health* 110, no. 2 (February 1, 2020): pp. 154–156. https://doi.org/10.2105/AJPH .2019.305468.

Shahbaz, A., & Funk, A. (n.d.). The Crisis of Social Media. Retrieved August 12, 2020, from https://freedomhouse.org/report/freedom-net/2019/crisis -social-media.

SplInternet. (2020, December 12). Retrieved December 16, 2020, from https://en.wikipedia.org/wiki/SplInternet.

Szentágotai-Tătar A, Miu AC (2017, January 25) Correction: Individual Differences in Emotion Regulation, Childhood Trauma and Proneness to Shame and Guilt in Adolescence. PLOS ONE 12(1): e0171151. https://doi.org/10.1371/journal.pone.0171151.

The Upcoming. (2020, March 04). The amazing story of Chatroulette. Retrieved August 3, 2020, from https://www.theupcoming.co.uk/2020 /03/04/the-amazing-story-of-chatroulette/.

Thorn, "Child Sex Trafficking Statistics." Retrieved August 9, 2020, from https://www.thorn.org/child-trafficking-statistics/.

US Department of Health and Human Services, Administration for Children, Youth and Families. (2014). Guidance to states and services on addressing human trafficking of children and youth in the United States. Washington, DC: Author. Available at http://www.acf.hhs.gov /sites/default/files/cb/acyf_human_trafficking_guidance.pdf.

Vogels, E., & Anderson, M. (2020, July 27). Americans and Digital Knowledge. Retrieved August 3, 2020, from https://www.pewre search.org/Internet/2019/10/09/americans-and-digital-knowledge/.

Walker S, Sanci L, Temple-Smith M. Sexting: Young women's and men's views on its nature and origins. *Journal of Adolescent Health*. 2013; 52: 697–701. 10.1016/j.jadohealth.2013.01.026.

Wikipedia. (2020, December 24). List of dangerous snakes. Retrieved August 3, 2020, from https://en.wikipedia.org/wiki/List_of_dangerous _snakes.

Willoughby, Brian J., Bonnie Young-Petersen, and Nathan D. Leonhardt. "Exploring Trajectories of Pornography Use Through Adolescence and Emerging Adulthood." *Journal of Sex Research* 55, no. 3 (March

2018): 297–309. doi:10.1080/00224499.2017.1368977. https://mash-able.com/article/pornhub-alternatives-free-porn-paid-porn/ Accessed August 14,2020.

Wilson, G. (2020, May 29). How Poisonous Are Coral Snakes? Retrieved August 3, 2020, from https://www.mysnakepet.com/how -poisonous-are-coral-snakes/.

Chapter 7

ABC News, (2006, January 6). Does The Matrix Inspire the Disturbed? Retrieved November 20, 2020, from https://abcnews.go.com/GMA/story?id=125158.

American Psychological Association. (2020, March 3) "APA Reaffirms Position on Violent Video Games and Violent Behavior." American Psychological Association. Retrieved April 28, 2020, from https://www.apa.org/news/press/releases/2020/03/violent-video-games-behavior.

Among Us - Apps on Google Play. (n.d.). Retrieved December 18, 2020, from https://play.google.com/store/apps/details?id=com.innersloth.spacemafia.

Centers for Disease Control and Prevention. "Childhood Obesity Facts." Centers for Disease Control and Prevention, Retrieved December 19, 2020, from https://www.cdc.gov/obesity/data/childhood.html.

Centers for Disease Control and Prevention. "How much physical activity do children need?" (2020, October 07). Retrieved December 18, 2020, from https://www.cdc.gov/physicalactivity/basics/children/index.htm.

Cooper, J. and Mackie, D. (1986). "Video Games and Aggression in Children." *Journal of Applied Social Psychology*, 16, 726–744.

Fung, B. (2020, September 28). Judge in Apple 'Fortnite' case slams Epic's tactics, hints at July trial date. Retrieved September 28, 2020, from https://www.cnn.com/2020/09/28/tech/apple-fortnite-epic-hearing/index.html.

Gartenberg, Chaim (July 17, 2020). "US video game spending hit a 10-year high in June". The Verge. Retrieved November 18, 2020.

Geek Insider, "Need A New Career? Top Professional Gamers Average The Yearly U.S. Salary In Under 6 Days," (2020, October 26). Retrieved December 20, 2020, from https://geekinsider.com/need-a-new-career -top-professional-gamers-average-the-yearly-u-s-salary-in-under -6-days/.

Gough, C. (2020, May 27). Global eSports audience 2020. Retrieved December 20, 2020, from https://www.statista.com/statistics/1109956 /global-esports-audience.

Hern, A. (2020, November 16). Video gaming can benefit mental health, find Oxford academics. Retrieved November 18, 2020, from https://www.theguardian.com/games/2020/nov/16/video-gaming-can -benefit-mental-health-find-oxford-academics.

Jamruk, K. (2017). The Weight Game: Fighting Childhood Obesity with Childhood Video Technology. *Journal of Legal Medicine*, 37(1/2), 175– 194. https://doi.org/10.1080/01947648.2017.1303409.

Markey, Patrick M., and Christopher J. Ferguson. *Moral Combat: Why the War on Violent Video Games Is Wrong*. Dallas, TX: BenBella Books, 2017.

Patchin, J. (2020, October 14). Tween Social Media and Gaming in 2020. Retrieved December 20, 2020, from https://cyberbullying.org /tween-social-media-and-gaming-2020.

Pei, Annie (April 30, 2020). "New Xbox on schedule but game production may be slowed by coronavirus, Microsoft exec says". *CNBC*. Retrieved May 8, 2020, from https://www.cnbc.com/2020/04/30/xbox-series-x-on-schedule-xbox-games-could-be-delayed-by-coronavirus.html.

Resolution on Violence in Video Games and Interactive Media. American Psychological Association, 2005. https://www.apa.org/about/policy /interactive-media.pdf.

Salen, K. (2020, September 28). Raising Good Gamers: New Report Tackles The Systemic Forces Shaping The Climate Of Online Play For Youth. Retrieved December 20, 2020, from https://clalliance .org/blog/raising-good-gamers-new-report-tackles-the-systemic -forces-shaping-the-climate-of-online-play-for-youth/.

The Common Sense Census: Media Use by Kids Age Zero to Eight, 2020: Common Sense Media. (2020, November 17). Retrieved November 20, 2020, from https://www.commonsensemedia.org/research/the-common-sense-census-media-use-by-kids-age-zero-to-eight-2020.

Tidy, J. (2019, July 28). US teenager wins $3m as Fortnite world champion. Retrieved December 20, 2020, from https://www.bbc.com/news /technology-49146644

Wenzel, J. (2020, November 09). Forget the PlayStation 5 or Xbox X Series: In 2020, you've got way more gaming options. Retrieved November

20, 2020, from https://theknow.denverpost.com/2020/11/09/vintage
-consoles-arcade-games-gaming/248317/.

Whittaker, Z. (2020, August 27). Discord says user abuse reports have doubled since last year. Retrieved December 20, 2020, from https://techcrunch.com/2020/08/27/discord-transparency-doubled/.

Chapter 8

American Views 2020: Trust, Media and Democracy. (2020, August 4). Retrieved December 27, 2020, from https://knightfoundation.org/reports/american-views-2020-trust-media-and-democracy/.

Andrews, E. (2013, December 17). 8 Things You May Not Know About Hammurabi's Code. Retrieved October 17, 2020, from https://www.history.com/news/8-things-you-may-not-know-about-hammurabis-code.

Big Three television networks. (2020, December 03). Retrieved October 15, 2020, from https://en.wikipedia.org/wiki/Big_Three_television_networks.

Braverman, A. (n.d.). History of Know Thyself. Retrieved October 21, 2020, from https://arkintime.com/know-thyself/history/.

Garrett, R. K., Bond, R., & Poulsen, S. (2020, September 03). Too many people think satirical news is real. Retrieved October 18, 2020, from https://theconversation.com/too-many-people-think-satirical-news-is-real-121666.

Judy, Cliff; Mendoza, Casey (February 22, 2018). "What Is 'Male Supremacy,' According To Southern Poverty Law Center?". WGBA-TV. Archived from the original on April 25, 2018. Accessed October 19, 2020.

Kirkpatrick, D. (2019, March 15). Massacre Suspect Traveled the World but Lived on the Internet. Retrieved October 18, 2020, from https://www.nytimes.com/2019/03/15/world/asia/new-zealand-shooting-brenton-tarrant.html.

Limor Shifman, Memes in a Digital World: Reconciling with a Conceptual Troublemaker, *Journal of Computer-Mediated Communication*, Volume 18, Issue 3, 1 April 2013, Pages 362–377, https://doi.org/10.1111/jcc4.12013.

New Survey Reveals Teens Get Their News from Social Media and YouTube: Common Sense Media. (2019, August 12). Retrieved October 15, 2020, from https://www.commonsensemedia.org/about-us/news

/press-releases/new-survey-reveals-teens-get-their-news-from-social -media-and-youtube.

Phillips, W. (2020, September 24). We Need to Talk About Talking About QAnon. Retrieved October 17, 2020, from https://www.wired.com /story/we-need-to-talk-about-talking-about-qanon/.

Skitka, L. J., Hanson, B. E., Morgan, G. S., & Wisneski, D. C. (in press). The psychology of moral conviction. *Annual Review of Psychology*, 72. Accessed October 21, 2020.

T. (2019, November 28). Conspiracy Theories. Retrieved October 15, 2020, from https://www.npr.org/2019/11/27/783307805/american-shadows.

Vosoughi, S., Roy, Deb & Aral, Sinan. (2018, March, 9) The spread of true and false news online. *Science*, 1146–1151.

Wood, J. (2020, February 17). These are the 10 biggest global health threats of the decade. Retrieved October 7, 2020, from https://www .weforum.org/agenda/2020/02/who-healthcare-challenges-2020s -climate-conflict-epidemics/.

Chapter 9

Federal Communications Commission, "2019 Broadband Deployment Report" (2019), Retrieved November 19, 2020, from https://www .fcc.gov/reports-research/reports/broadband-progress-reports/2019 -broadband-deployment-report.

Lombana-Bermudez, Andres, Sandra Cortesi, et. al. (2020) "Youth and the Digital Economy: Exploring Youth Practices, Motivations, Skills, Pathways, and Value Creation," Youth and Media, Berkman Klein Center for Internet & Society. Retrieved from https://cyber.harvard .edu/publication/2020/youth-and-digital-economy.

Microsoft, "Microsoft Airband: An Update on Connecting Rural America," (2019, October 17), Retrieved November 19, 2020, from https://news .microsoft.com/rural-broadband.

Pate, Deanna. "The Skills Companies Need Most in 2020-And How to Learn Them." LinkedIn Learning. Retrieved November 9, 2020, from https://learning.linkedin.com/blog/top-skills/the-skills -companies-need-most-in-2020and-how-to-learn-them.

UCLA Center for Neighborhood Knowledge. (2020, October 28). COVID-19 and the Digital Divide in Virtual Learning. Retrieved November

9, 2020, from https://knowledge.luskin.ucla.edu/2020/10/28/covid-19 -and-the-digital-divide-in-virtual-learning/.

Van Nuys, A. (2020, October 14). Top 10 Takeaways from the LinkedIn Learning Virtual Summit. Retrieved November 9, 2020, from https://www.linkedin.com/business/learning/blog/learning-and -development/top-10-takeaways-from-linkedin-learning-virtual -summit-2020.

Vogels, E. A. (2020, September 10). 59% of U.S. parents with lower incomes say their child may face digital obstacles in schoolwork. Retrieved November 19, 2020, from https://www.pewresearch .org/fact-tank/2020/09/10/59-of-u-s-parents-with-lower-incomes -say-their-child-may-face-digital-obstacles-in-schoolwork/.

Index